THE
PLECTRUM
BANJO
CHORD BIBLE

(CGBD Standard Tuning)

by

Tobe A. Richards

A Fretted Friends Publication for Cabot Books

Published by:
Cabot Books
Copyright © 2007 & 2016 by Cabot Books
All rights reserved.

First Edition October 2007
Second Edition February 2016

ISBN-13: 978-1-906207-37-3

Cabot Books
3 Kenton Mews
Henleaze
Bristol
BS9 4LT
United Kingdom

Visit our online site at www.frettedfriendsmusic.com
e-mail: cabotbooks@blueyonder.co.uk

TABLE OF CONTENTS

INTRODUCTION

The Plectrum Banjo Chord Bible provides the musician with 1,728 chords in all keys, featuring 68 different chord types, with 3 variations of each standard chord. 144 major slash chords are also included, together with 48 moveable chord shape diagrams (providing access to a further 576 barré and standard moveable chords) making this the most comprehensive reference guide for the plectrum banjo currently available. For many years now, guitarists have been able to pick up a songbook and instantly play the songs in front of them, either with the help of one of the many published guides, or through the chord boxes supplied with most popular music. With the help of this *Chord Bible*, beginners and experienced plectrum banjo players alike will be able to take advantage of the many songbooks, fake books and musical compendiums by any artist you would care to name, from *The Beatles* to *Joan Baez*, from *Planxty* to *The Pogues* or *Springsteen* to *Simon & Garfunkel*. With 68 different chordal variations in all keys, virtually any song should be playable!

Having a good chordal knowledge should arguably be the bedrock in any fretted or keyboard musicians armoury. Whether you're playing rock, pop, folk, jazz, blues, country or other types of music, it's impossible to supply a suitable accompaniment to any vocal or solo instrumental music without providing a chordal or harmonic backing. The subtle nuance of an added ninth chord over a major chord is something that can't be captured simply by playing a melody line. In theory it is possible to approximate the harmonic intervals of any music using a limited palette of chords - probably around ten to twelve. But wherever possible it's best to use correct harmonies if they're available to you.

Having four strings, the plectrum banjo is obviously limited to four note chords, but by making acceptable compromises and omitting the least important parts of that chord, even the most complex musical structures are possible. For instance, in the case of an eleventh, the third is generally omitted without the character of the chord being adversely affected. Equally, the root or key note isn't always necessary to achieve an effective approximation of the full chord. The third is rarely missing from the majority of chords (other than elevenths) as it determines whether the key is major or minor - although this isn't a hard and fast rule, particularly in folk music where the root and fifth form the basis of most traditional music. These two intervals are generally the starting point for a number of open tunings of instruments as diverse as the guitar, the Irish bouzouki and the mountain dulcimer. The same interval is also used in a lot of heavy rock where a fifth chord is described as a *power chord*. Even though a power chord is technically neither major nor minor, it's more often used as an alternative for a major chord in most popular music.

One question which often pops up is *how many chords do I need to learn?* The smart answer is *'how long is a piece of string?'*, which is true, but it doesn't actually answer the question if you don't know where to start. My advice would be to begin with simple chord clusters like the popular G, C, D and Em progression and gradually work in new ones as you advance. If you intend playing within a rock format, it's probably sensible to learn the E, A, B sequence which is the staple of most guitarists and bassists. As a generalisation, jazz probably requires the greatest chordal knowledge of any form of music, so the learning curve will be longer if you're planning to pick up any songbook and instantly produce a recognisable version of your favourite *Duke Ellington* or *Steely Dan* number. The only truth as far as harmonic knowledge goes is you can never learn *too* much!

In this series of chord theory books, I've included a comprehensive selection of configurations of chords in all keys. As I mentioned previously, this will enable you to pick up virtually any songbook or fake book (topline melody and chord symbols) and look up the chord shape that's needed. Obviously, you'll come across the occasional song which doesn't conform to the normal harmonic intervals which you find in this, or any other chord theory publication, but with a little experimentation and experience, you'll be able to make a reasonable stab at it. For instance, most players would be more than a little bemused if they suddenly came across an instruction to play a *Gbmaj7add6/D*. Fortunately, this is fairly unusual, but from the knowledge you'll have learned, you'll be able to use a similar chord or work it out note by note. Put simply, if every theoretically possible chord shape were to be included in this or any other book, the result would resemble something akin to several volumes of the *Yellow Pages*!

FINGERING

Always a tricky subject and one which seems to generate a lot of discussion and differing opinions as to which method is correct. Personally, I take the view that it's a largely fruitless exercise, as the number of variables involved make a definitive answer unlikely. So what I've decided to do in this book is to choose fingering positions which feel comfortable to me. Some chord shapes will dictate the fingering used, but others will be down to personal preference. If you can practise your two and three finger chords using different fingers, it will make your playing a lot more fluid when you change to another chord shape. But if you develop habits which limit you to one playing position, it isn't the end of the world either, if you can make the transitions seamless.

The only rules, if you could loosely call them that, are:-

a) Don't abandon using your pinky or little finger if you're just beginning to play, as you'll eventually need it for some of the four finger chords which frequently crop up.

b) Try to avoid fretting with the thumb unless you're learning an instrument like the mountain dulcimer which requires a longer stretch. I know a number of players employ it on slimmer necked instruments, but I personally feel it leads to bad habits.

c) Keep your left hand fingernails short or fretting becomes a major problem. Obviously do the reverse if you're a lefty.

d) If you're a beginner and you're naturally left handed, don't get persuaded into buying a right handed instrument - it won't work! The learning curve will be steeper and you'll never get the fluidity you'd achieve with your natural hand. Most acoustic instruments can be adapted for a left hander apart from cutaway guitars and f-style mandolins etc., by reversing the nut and strings. For the non-reversible instruments, always go for a left handed model.

e) Learn to barré with other fingers apart from your index finger. This will prove invaluable with more complex chords and increase finger strength as well.

f) Don't be afraid to use fingerings further up the neck in combination with open strings as these will give you interesting new voicings and are generally quite popular in folk music. A number of these are provided in this book.

g) The plectrum banjo is generally played with a pick or plectrum. Alternatively, fingerpicks or fingernails can be used if you're accustomed to this method of playing. Using a pick generally produces a much brighter sound with more attack.

CHORD THEORY & FAQs

Q   *What is a chord?*

A   It's a collection of three or more notes played simultaneously. The exceptions in this book are the fourths and fifths (power chords) which aren't in the strictest sense, true chords. For convenience sake, they are classed as such.

Q   *What is a triad?*

A   A chord containing three notes. For example, G Major, Bm, D+ or Asus4.

Q   *What are intervals?*

A   Intervals are the musical distance between notes in a musical scale. For instance in the scale of C Major, C is the 1st note, D is the 2nd note, E the 3rd and so on. So if you're playing the chord of C Major, your intervals will be 1–3–5 or C as the *first* note, E as the *third* note and G as the *perfect fifth*.

Q   *What is a chromatic scale and which intervals does it contain?*

A: A chromatic scale encompasses all twelve notes in a musical scale, including the sharps and flats. It's also the basis for the naming of *every* chord in existence. See the staff diagram below to see the intervals:

Chromatic Scale in C

Root or 1st	Minor 2nd	Major 2nd	Minor 3rd	Major 3rd	Perfect 4th	Augmented 4th	*or*	Diminished 5th	Perfect 5th	Minor 6th	Major 6th	Minor 7th	Major 7th

Q   *What is a seventh chord?*

A: In its most basic form, an additional note beyond the triad. Sevenths can be either major or flattened. For instance, returning to our old friend, the key of C, a Cmaj7 has an added B on top of the C–E–G triad. The resultant chord has a mellow quality often found in jazz. Now if you take the B and flatten it by dropping the fourth note in your chord down to a B flat, you get a C7.

Q: *Then why isn't it called a C minor seventh?*

A: Technically this *is* a minor seventh note, but this would create a lot of confusion when naming chords, as you already have a minor interval option in your triad (in the key of C major, E flat), so it's always referred to as a 7th to differentiate between it and a major seventh.

Q: *What is an extension?*

A: A chord which goes beyond the scope of triads and sevenths. Basically, extensions are additional notes placed above the triad or seventh in a musical stave, fingerboard or keyboard. It's important to understand these are, for theoretical purposes, always placed above the seventh. Or in layman's terms, higher up the scale. The confusion comes when you start to realise a 9th is identical to a 2nd - in the scale of C – a D note.

Q: *So why is the ninth note the same as the second note?*

A: This takes a little grasping, but if you remember that if your note goes higher than the seventh it's a 9th, but if it's lower, it'll be a 2nd. An example of this would be Csus2, which contains the root note of C, a 2nd or suspended D note and a G, the perfect 5th. You'll see this even more clearly if you look at the piano keyboard diagram below. Count from the C up to the following D beyond the 7th (B note). From the C to the second D is exactly nine whole notes.

Q: *Do any other extensions share a common note?*

A: Yes, other examples include the *11th*, which is also a *4th* and the *13th* which shares a note with the *6th*.

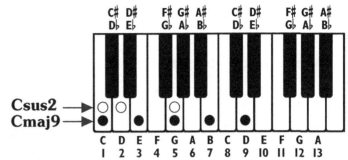

Q: *What are inversions?*

A: In the root version of a chord, the notes run in their correct order from lowest to highest. In the case of G major, it would be G–B–D. With an inversion of the same chord the notes would run in a different order. For example, the first inversion of G major would be B–D–G and the second, D–G–B. In general, triads sound more or less the same when they're inverted, but that's certainly not the case with sevenths and extensions which can sound quite different and occasionally discordant when the notes are jumbled up in certain configurations. Inversions can also produce different chords using the same basic notes. A good example of this would be C6 (C-E-G-A) which produces an Am7 (A-C-E-G) when it's inverted (both contain the notes of C–E–G–A, but in a different order). The major variations are in the tonal properties of the chords, making them sound quite different from one another.

Q: *Do elevenths and thirteenths have any particular properties?*

A: Yes. In most cases the 3rd is omitted from eleventh chords and the 11th from the majority of thirteenths as they're deemed unnecessary and arguably, create unwanted dissonance.

Q: *Some chords are called by different names in different music books. What should I do?*

A: The alternative chord name reference chart at the back of the book should help sort out the confusion.

Q: *What is a suspended chord?*

A: It's simpler to think of suspended chords as a stepping stone to a major or resolving chord. In effect the third has been left in a state of suspension by either raising it to a fourth (sus4) or lowering it to a second (sus2). Sevenths also provide versions of the suspended chord in the form of C7sus4 or C7sus2 (using the key of C as an example).

Q: *What is a diminished chord?*

A: A diminished chord has a dissonent quality to it where the third and fifth notes in a triad are flattened by a semi-tone. Again, using C as an example, C major (C-E-G) is altered to Cdim (C-E♭-G♭). A second version of a dimished chord is also used in many forms of music, the diminished seventh. This retains the elements of a standard diminished chord, adding a double flat in the seventh (C-E♭-G♭-B♭♭). A B♭♭ in this case is, to all intents and purposes, really an A note.

Q: *What is an augmented chord?*

A: An augmented chord basically performs the opposite task to a diminished one. Instead of lowering the fifth by a semitone, it raises it by the same interval. A C+ (augmented) chord contains the triad of C-E-G♯. The major root and third are retained and the fifth is sharpened.

UNDERSTANDING THE CHORD BOXES

The three diagrams below show the chord conventions illustrated in this guide. Most experienced fretted instrument players should be familiar with them. The suggested fingering positions are only meant as a general guide and will depend, in many instances, on hand size, finger length and flexibility, so feel free to experiment. The location of the black circles is unalterable, though, if you want to produce the correct voicing.

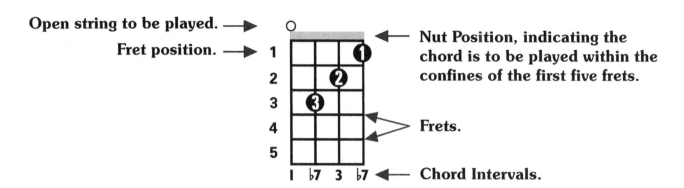

Open string to be played. ⟶

Fret position. ⟶

Nut Position, indicating the chord is to be played within the confines of the first five frets.

Frets.

Chord Intervals.

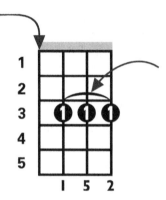

If there are no markers above or below the string, the string should not be played.

Barré chord (in this example, a three string barré to be fretted with the index finger).

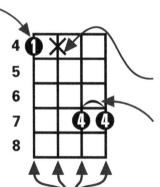

Suggested fingering. In this case the 1st or index finger marker is displayed.

A damped string. In this example the 3rd string should be damped using the lower pad of the middle finger, fretting the 4th string.

A two string barré to be played with the fourth finger.

Left to right: 4th, 3rd, 2nd and 1st courses of strings.

Whether a fretted instrument has single strings or pairs of strings, the chord boxes in this book, other chord dictionaries and songbooks treat it as a four stringed instrument. This convention is common to all double or triple course instruments such as the mandolin or tiple, making the diagrams a lot less confusing and free from unnecessary clutter.

PLECTRUM BANJO
FINGERBOARD & TUNING LAYOUT

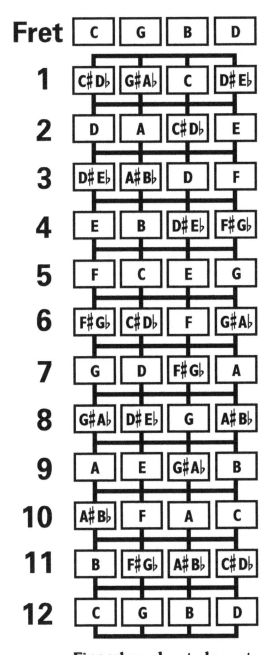

Fingerboard note layout

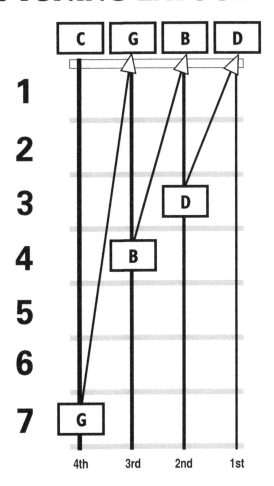

Tuning the plectrum banjo by fretting at given intervals on the fingerboard

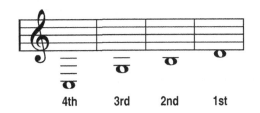

Plectrum banjo CGBD tuning in standard notation

To tune your plectrum banjo accurately, it's best to use an electronic chromatic tuner, but if there isn't one available, you can tune it to a guitar or piano/electronic keyboard. The following tuning grid gives the correct fingering positions on the guitar fingerboard and piano keyboard.

Plectrum Banjo	Guitar	Piano
1st String (D)	2nd string (B) fretted at the 3rd fret	1st D above middle C
2nd String (B)	2nd open string (B)	1st B below middle C
3rd String (G)	3rd open string (G)	1st G below middle C
4th String (C)	5th string (A) fretted at the 3rd fret	1st C below middle C

THE CHORDS COVERED IN THIS BOOK

Chord	Chord Name in Full	Harmonic Interval
C	Major	1–3–5
Cm	Minor	1–F3-5
C-5	Major Diminished Fifth	1–3–F5
C°	Diminished	1–F3—F5
C4	Fourth	1–4
C5	Fifth or Power Chord	1–5
Csus2	Suspended Second	1–2–5
Csus4	Suspended Fourth	1–4–5
Csus4add9	Suspended Fourth Added Ninth	1–4–5–9
C+	Augmented	1–3–S5
C6	Major Sixth	1–3–5–6
Cadd9	Major Added Ninth	1–3–5–9
Cadd11	Major Added Eleventh	1–3–5–11
Cm6	Minor Sixth	1–F3–5–6
Cm-6	Minor Diminished Sixth	1–F3–5–F6
Cmadd9	Minor Added Ninth	1–F3–5–9
C6add9	Major Sixth Added Ninth	1–3–5–6–9
Cm6add9	Minor Sixth Added Ninth	1–F3–5–6–9
C°7	Diminished Seventh	1–F3–F5–DF7
C7	Seventh	1–3–5–F7
C7sus2	Seventh Suspended Second	1–2–5–F7
C7sus4	Seventh Suspended Fourth	1–4–5–F7
C7-5	Seventh Diminished Fifth	1–3–F5–F7
C7+5	Seventh Augmented Fifth	1–3–S5–F7
C7-9	Seventh Minor Ninth	1–3–5–F7–F9
C7+9	Seventh Augmented Ninth	1–3–5–F7–S9
C7-5-9	Seventh Diminished Fifth Minor Ninth	1–3–F5–F7–F9
C7-5+9	Seventh Diminished Fifth Augmented Ninth	1–3–F5–F7–S9
C7+5-9	Seventh Augmented Fifth Minor Ninth	1–3–S5–F7–F9
C7+5+9	Seventh Augmented Fifth Augmented Ninth	1–3–S5–F7–S9
C7add11	Seventh Added Eleventh	1–3–5–F7–11
C7+11	Seventh Augmented Eleventh	1–3–5–F7–S11
C7add13	Seventh Added Thirteenth	1–3–5–F7–13
Cm7	Minor Seventh	1–F3–5–F7
Cm7-5	Minor Seventh Diminished Fifth	1–F3–F5–F7
Cm7-5-9	Minor Seventh Diminished Fifth Minor Ninth	1–F3–F5–F7–F9
Cm7-9	Minor Seventh Minor Ninth	1–F3–5–F7–F9
Cm7add11	Minor Seventh Added Eleventh	1–F3–5–F7–11
Cm(maj7)	Minor Major Seventh	1–F3–5–7
Cmaj7	Major Seventh	1–3–5–7
Cmaj7-5	Major Seventh Diminished Fifth	1–3–F5–7
Cmaj7+5	Major Seventh Augmented Fifth	1–3–S5–7
Cmaj7+11	Major Seventh Augmented Eleventh	1–3–5–7–S11
C9	Ninth	1–3–5–F7–9
C9sus4	Ninth Suspended Fourth	1–4–5–F7–9
C9-5	Ninth Diminished Fifth	1–3–F5–F7–9
C9+5	Ninth Augmented Fifth	1–3–S5–F7–9
C9+11	Ninth Augmented Eleventh	1–3–5–F7–9–S11
Cm9	Minor Ninth	1–F3–5–F7–9

Chord	Chord Name in Full	Harmonic Interval
Cm9-5	Minor Ninth Diminished Fifth	1–F3–F5–F7–9
Cm(maj9)	Minor Major Ninth	1–F3–5–7–9
Cmaj9	Major Ninth	1–3–5–7–9
Cmaj9-5	Major Ninth Diminished Fifth	1–3–F5–7–9
Cmaj9+5	Major Ninth Augmented Fifth	1–3–S5–7–9
Cmaj9add6	Major Ninth Added Sixth	1–3–5–6–7–9
Cmaj9+11	Major Ninth Augmented Eleventh	1–3–5–7–9–S11
C11	Eleventh	1–3–5–F7–9–11
C11-9	Eleventh Diminished Ninth	1–3–5–F7–F9–11
Cm11	Minor Eleventh	1–F3–5–F7–9–11
Cmaj11	Major Eleventh	1–3–5–7–9–11
C13	Thirteenth	1–3–5–F7–9–11–13
C13sus4	Thirteenth Suspended Fourth	1–4–5–F7–9–11–13
C13-5-9	Thirteenth Diminished Fifth Minor Ninth	1–3–F5–F7–F9–11–13
C13-9	Thirteenth Minor Ninth	1–3–5–F7–F9–11–13
C13+9	Thirteenth Augmented Ninth	1–3–5–F7–S9–11–13
C13+11	Thirteenth Augmented Eleventh	1–3–5–F7–9–S11–13
Cm13	Minor Thirteenth	1–F3–5–F7–9–11–13
Cmaj13	Major Thirteenth	1–3–5–7–9–11–13

Key: F = Flat   S = Sharp   DF = Double Flat

SLASH CHORDS

What is a slash chord? Put simply, they're standard chords with an added note in the bass. *So what differentiates a C chord from a C/G when the G is already part of that chord, in this case, the fifth?* Theoretically, nothing, but the difference is very apparent when you actually sound the chord. The G bass is emphasised to provide a different feel to the harmonics. Slashes are also commonly found when the music calls for a descending bassline. For example; C, C/B, C/A and C/G.

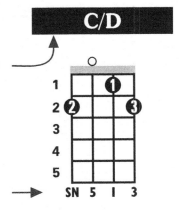

The note after the slash indicates the bass note being played. For instance C/D would be an instruction to play a C chord with a D bass.

Slash Note. Generally found on the 5th & 4th courses.

How do I play a slash chord that isn't listed in this book? Well, firstly, it would be an almost impossible task to cover every possible slash chord in existence, because the variations are potentially even greater than with standard chords. What you can do, within the confines of this guide, is to find the part of the chord before the slash in the main body of the book and then look for the nearest bass note on the third or fourth course (strings 3 to 4). To find the right bass note, consult the fingerboard layout on *page 9*.

USING A CAPO (OR *CAPO D'ASTRA*)

Using a capo is a quick and easy way of changing key to suit a different vocal range or to join in with with other musicians playing in a different key. For the uniniated, a capo is a moveable bar that clamps onto the fingerboard of fretted instruments. It works in much the same way as using a finger barré to hold down the strings. They come in a variety of designs and prices, the simplest using a metal rod covered in rubber and sprung with elastic. For the plectrum banjo, look for a dedicated banjo capo.

C Chords

C	Cm	C7	Cm7

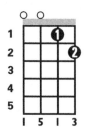 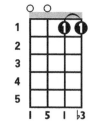 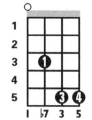 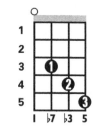

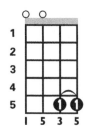 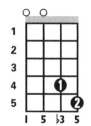 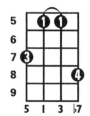 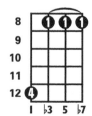

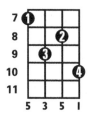 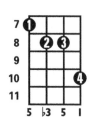 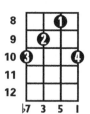 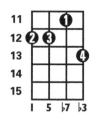

C5	C6	Cm6	Cmaj7

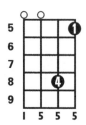 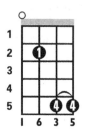 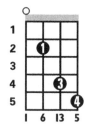 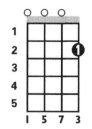

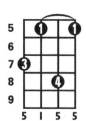 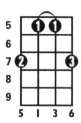 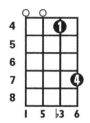 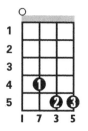

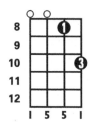 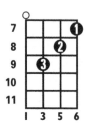 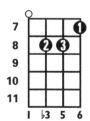 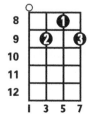

C Chords

Cº

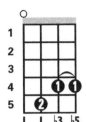

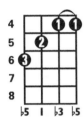

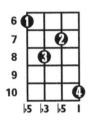

Cº7

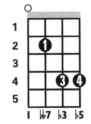

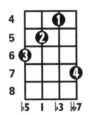

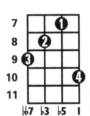

C-5

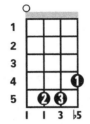

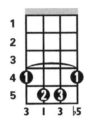

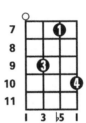

C+

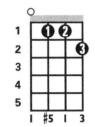

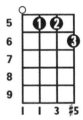

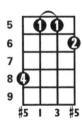

Csus2

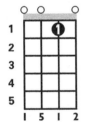

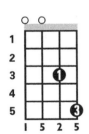

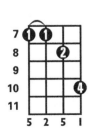

Csus4

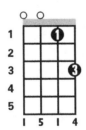

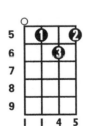

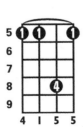

C7sus4

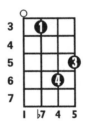

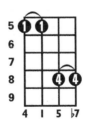

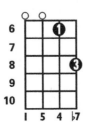

Cm7-5

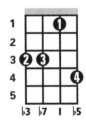

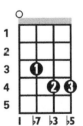

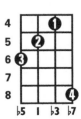

13

C Chords

Cadd9

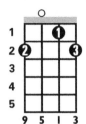

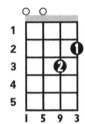

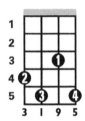

Cmadd9

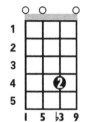

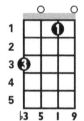

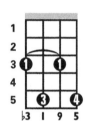

C6add9

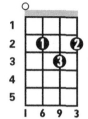

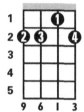

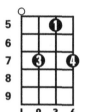

Cm6add9

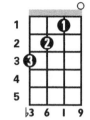

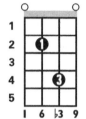

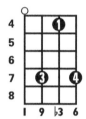

C7-5

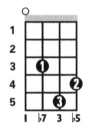

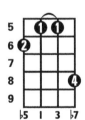

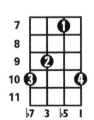

C7+5

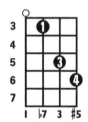

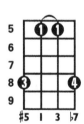

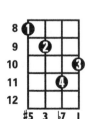

C7-9

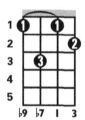

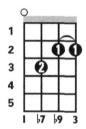

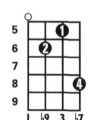

C7+9

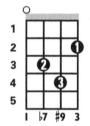

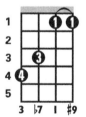

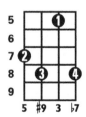

14

C Chords

Cm(maj7)

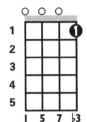

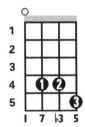

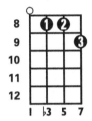

Cmaj7-5

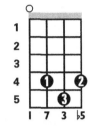

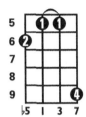

Cmaj7+5

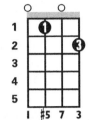

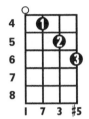

C9

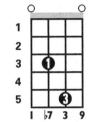

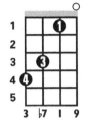

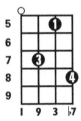

Cm9

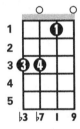

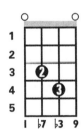

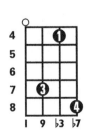

Cmaj9

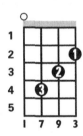

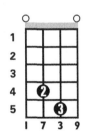

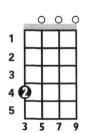

C11

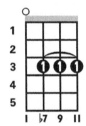

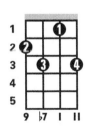

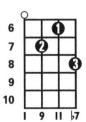

C13

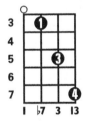

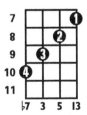

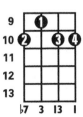

15

C Chords (Advanced)

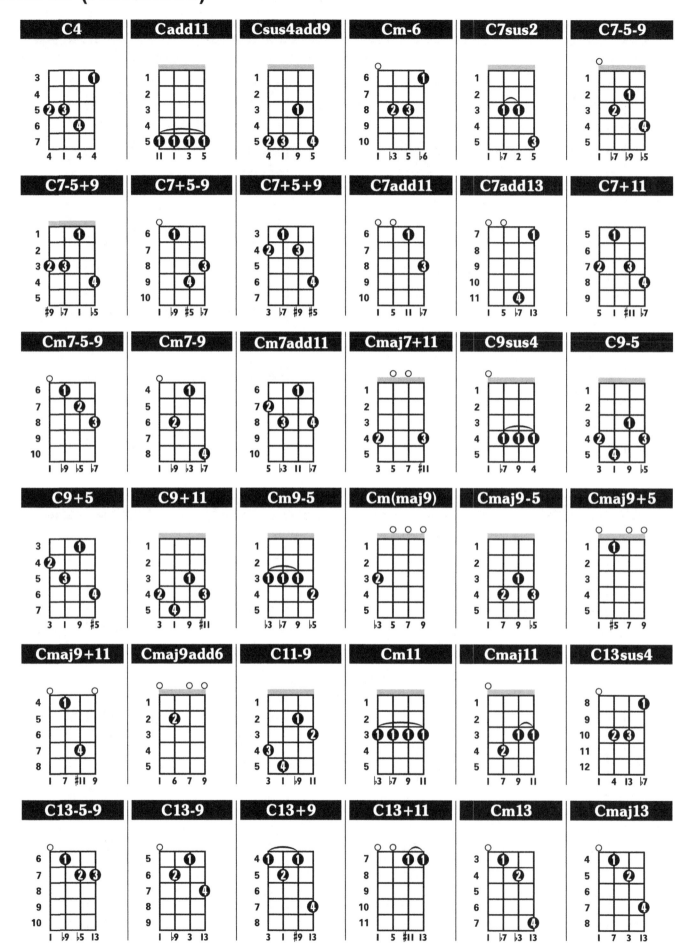

D♭

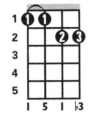

D♭m

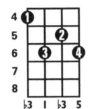

D♭7

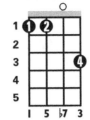

D♭m7

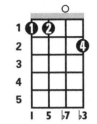

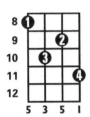

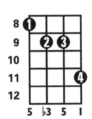

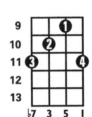

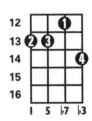

D♭5

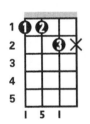

D♭6

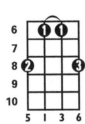

D♭m6

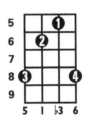

D♭maj7

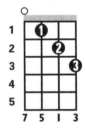

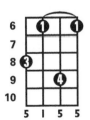

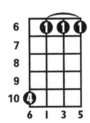

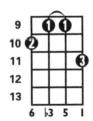

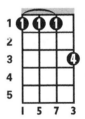

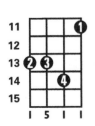

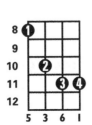

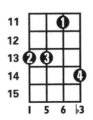

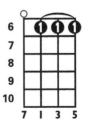

C#/ D♭ Chords

D♭°	D♭°7	D♭-5	D♭+

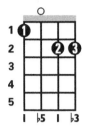
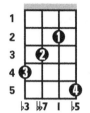
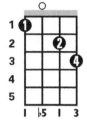
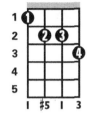

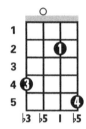
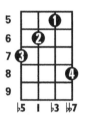
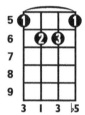
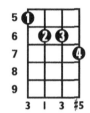

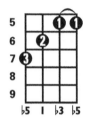
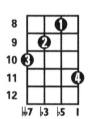
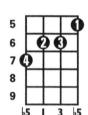
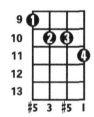

D♭sus2	D♭sus4	D♭7sus4	D♭m7-5

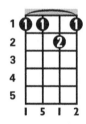
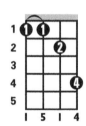
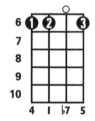
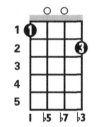

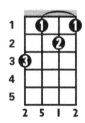
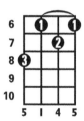
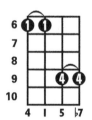
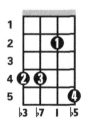

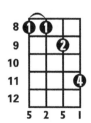
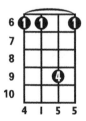
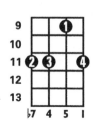
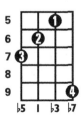

D♭add9

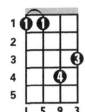
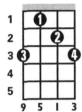
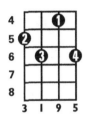

D♭madd9

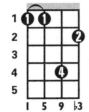
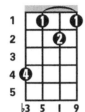
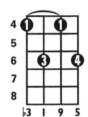

D♭6add9

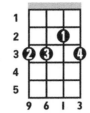
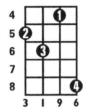
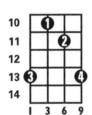

D♭m6add9

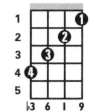
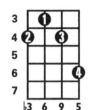
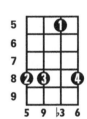

D♭7-5

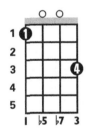
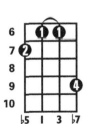
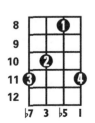

D♭7+5

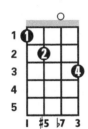
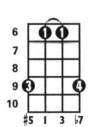
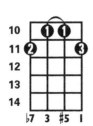

D♭7-9

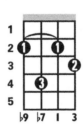
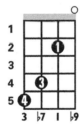
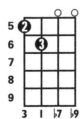

D♭7+9

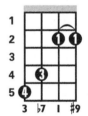
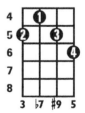
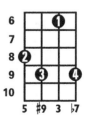

19

C#/ Db Chords

Dbm(maj7)
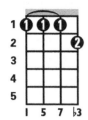
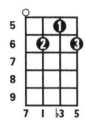
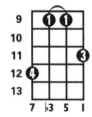

Dbmaj7-5
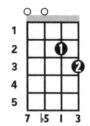
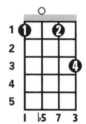
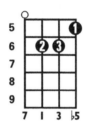

Dbmaj7+5
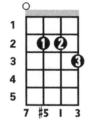
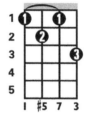
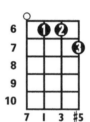

Db9
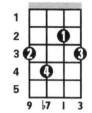
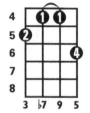
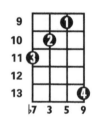

Dbm9
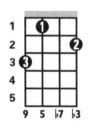
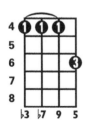
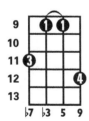

Dbmaj9
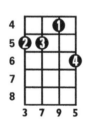
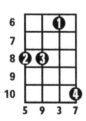
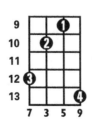

Db11
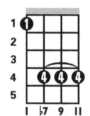
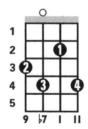
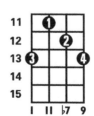

Db13
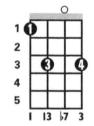
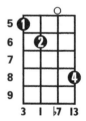
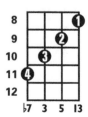

20

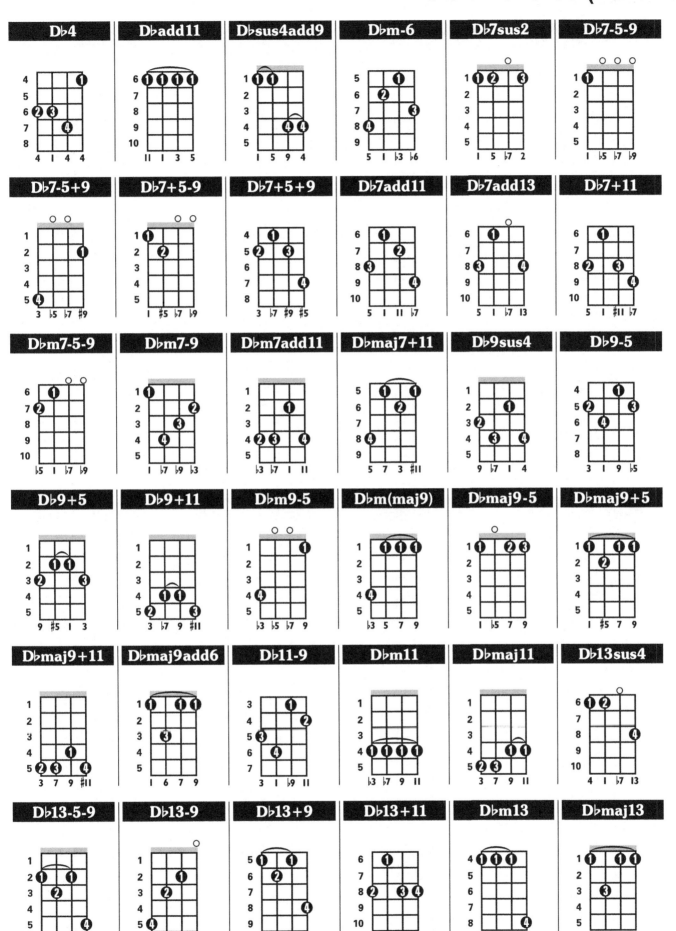

D Chords

D	**Dm**	**D7**	**Dm7**
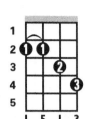	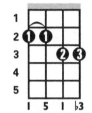	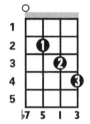	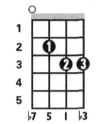
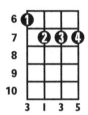	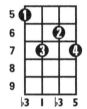	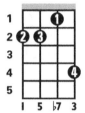	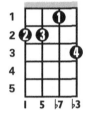
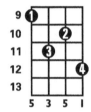	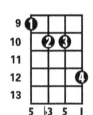	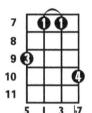	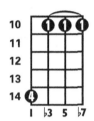

D5	**D6**	**Dm6**	**Dmaj7**
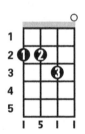	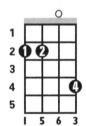	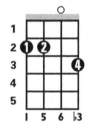	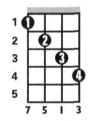
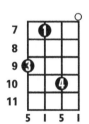	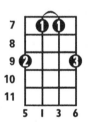	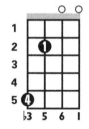	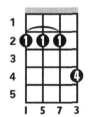
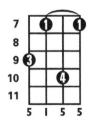	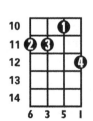	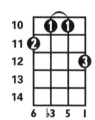	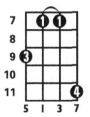

D Chords

D°

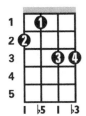

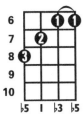

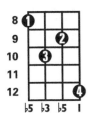

D°7

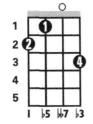

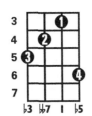

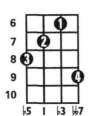

D-5

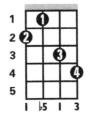

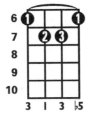

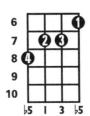

D+

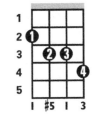

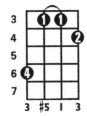

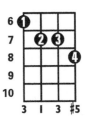

Dsus2

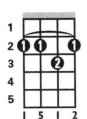

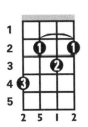

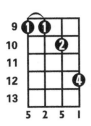

Dsus4

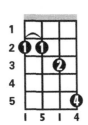

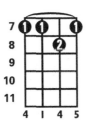

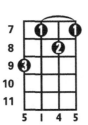

D7sus4

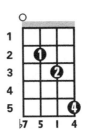

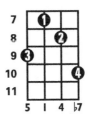

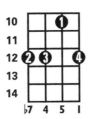

Dm7-5

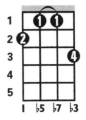

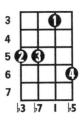

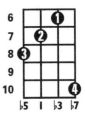

23

D Chords

Dadd9	Dmadd9	D6add9	Dm6add9
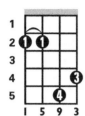	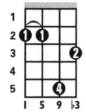	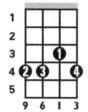	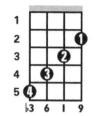
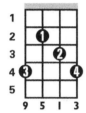	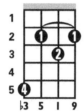	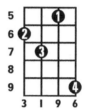	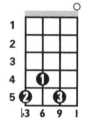
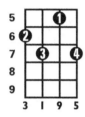	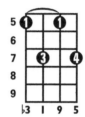	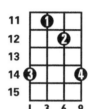	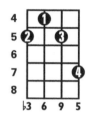

D7-5	D7+5	D7-9	D7+9
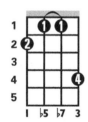	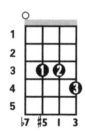	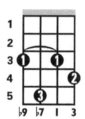	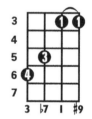
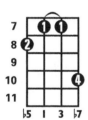	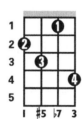	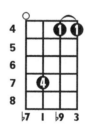	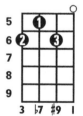
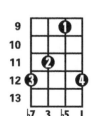	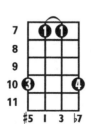	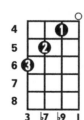	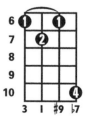

D Chords

Dm(maj7)
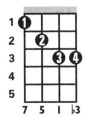
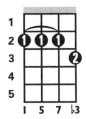
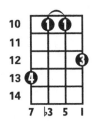

Dmaj7-5
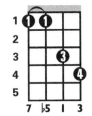
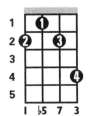
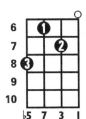

Dmaj7+5
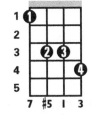
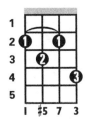

D9
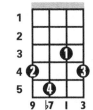
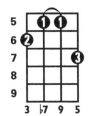
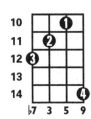

Dm9
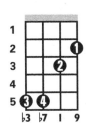
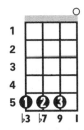
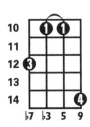

Dmaj9
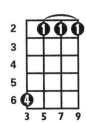
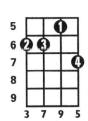
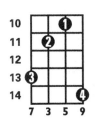

D11
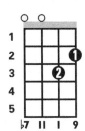
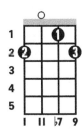
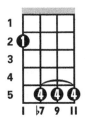

D13
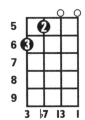
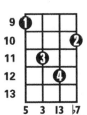
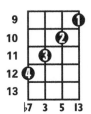

25

D Chords (Advanced)

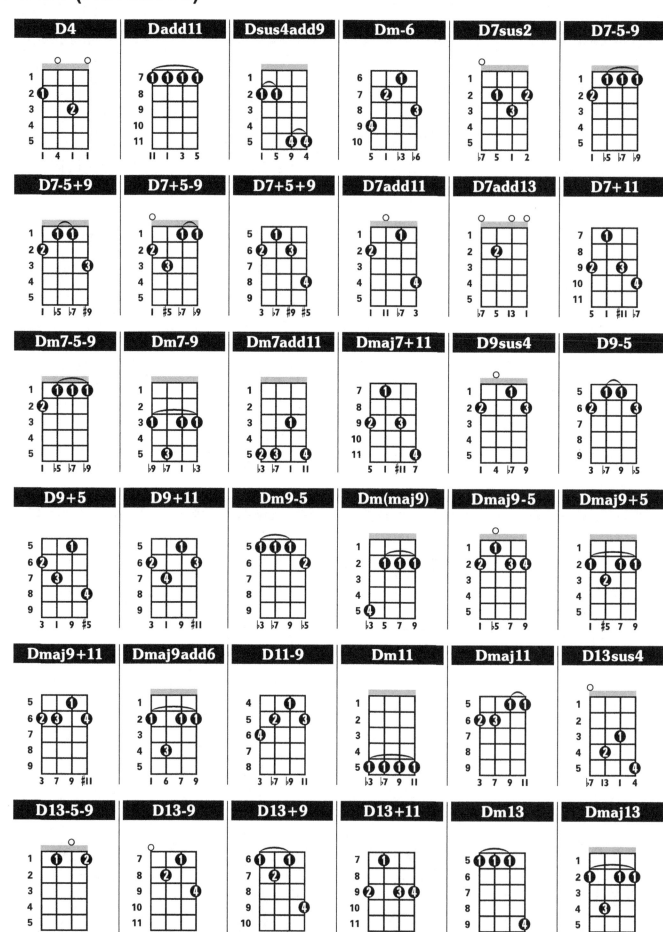

E♭
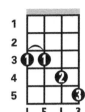
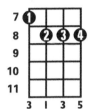
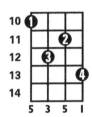

E♭m
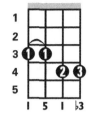
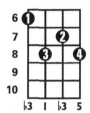
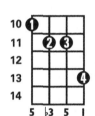

E♭7
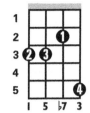
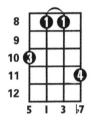
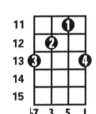

E♭m7
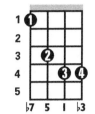
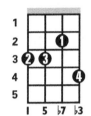
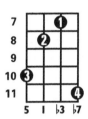

E♭5
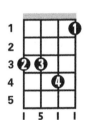
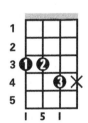
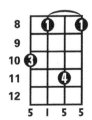

E♭6
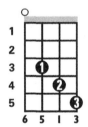
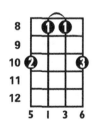
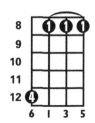

E♭m6
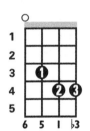
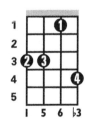
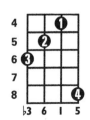

E♭maj7
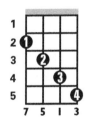
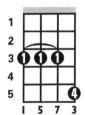
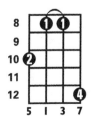

D#/ E♭ Chords

E♭°

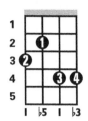

E♭°7

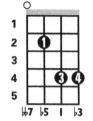

E♭-5

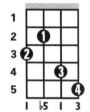

E♭+

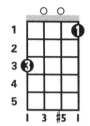

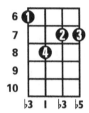

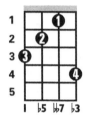

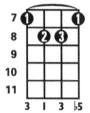

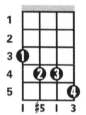

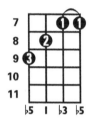

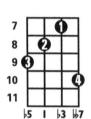

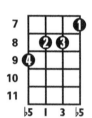

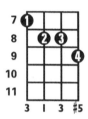

E♭sus2

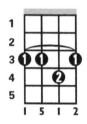

E♭sus4

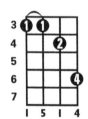

E♭7sus4

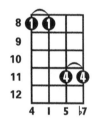

E♭m7-5

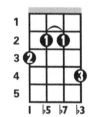

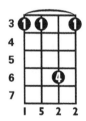

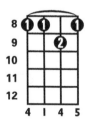

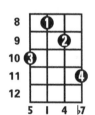

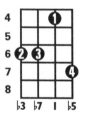

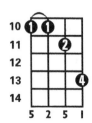

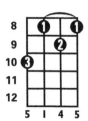

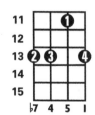

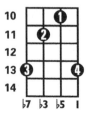

E♭add9

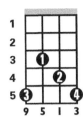

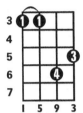

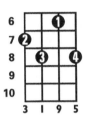

E♭madd9

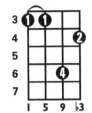

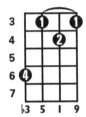

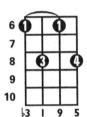

E♭6add9

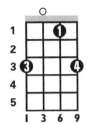

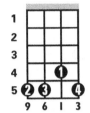

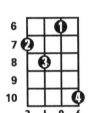

E♭m6add9

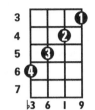

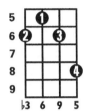

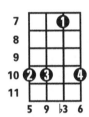

E♭7-5

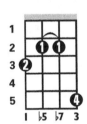

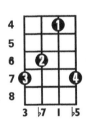

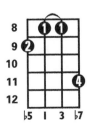

E♭7+5

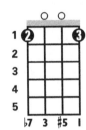

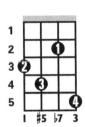

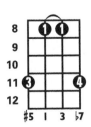

E♭7-9

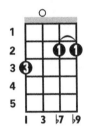

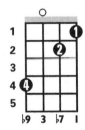

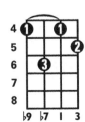

E♭7+9

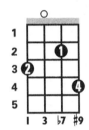

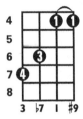

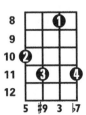

D#/ Eb Chords

Ebm(maj7)
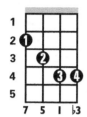
7 5 1 b3

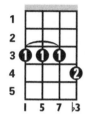
1 5 7 b3

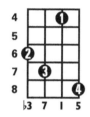
b3 7 1 5

Ebmaj7-5
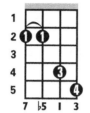
7 b5 1 3

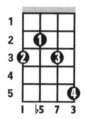
1 b5 7 3

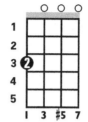
b5 1 3 7

Ebmaj7+5
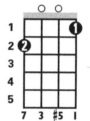
1 3 #5 7

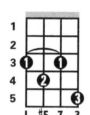
7 3 #5 1

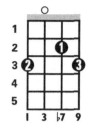
1 #5 7 3

Eb9
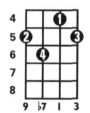
1 3 b7 9

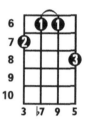
9 b7 1 3

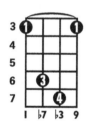
3 b7 9 5

Ebm9
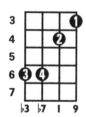
1 b7 b3 9

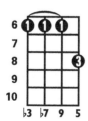
b3 b7 1 9

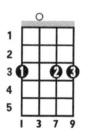
b3 b7 9 5

Ebmaj9
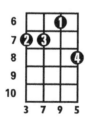
1 3 7 9

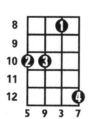
3 7 9 5

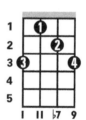
5 9 3 7

Eb11
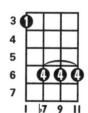
1 11 b7 9

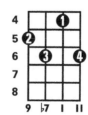
1 b7 9 11

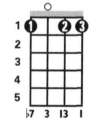
9 b7 1 11

Eb13
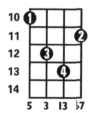
b7 3 13 1

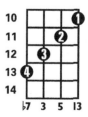
5 3 13 b7

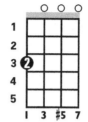
b7 3 5 13

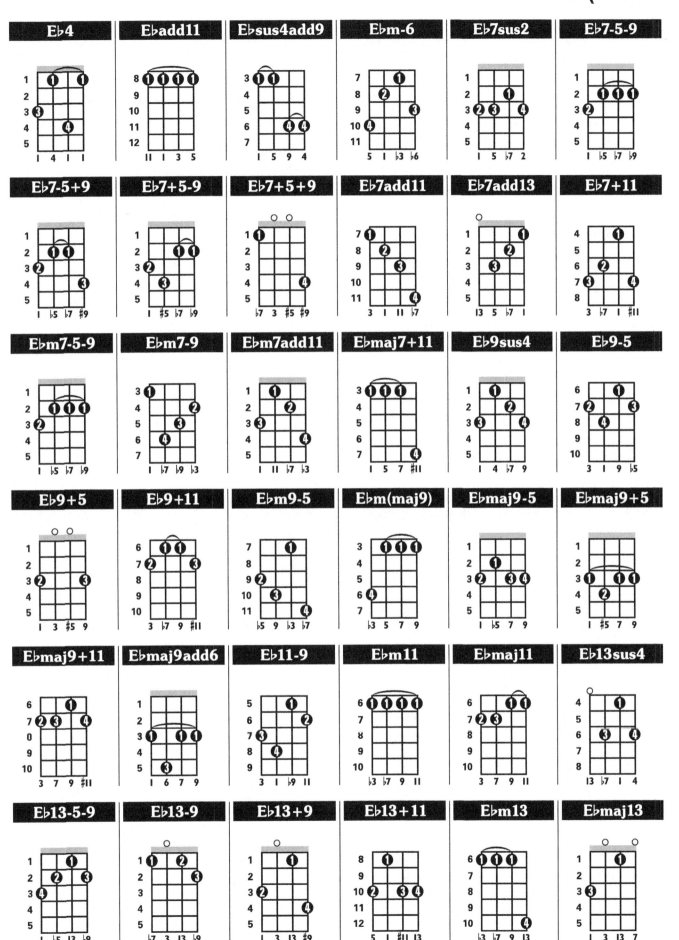

E Chords

E	Em	E7	Em7
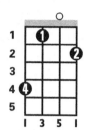	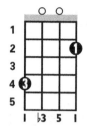	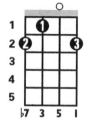	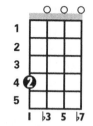
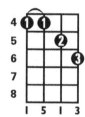	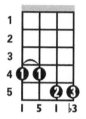	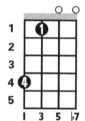	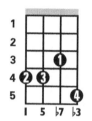
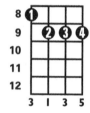	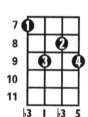	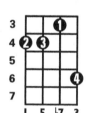	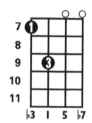

E5	E6	Em6	Emaj7
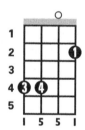	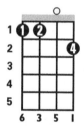	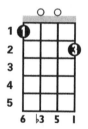	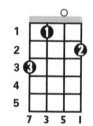
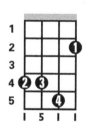	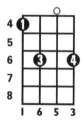	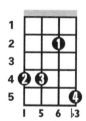	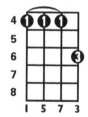
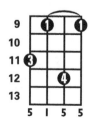	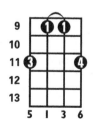	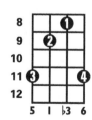	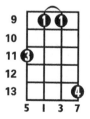

E°

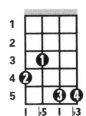

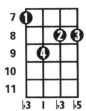

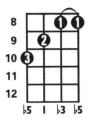

E°7

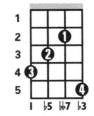

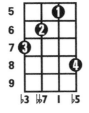

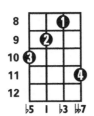

E-5

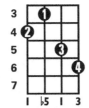

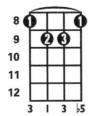

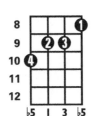

E+

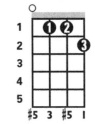

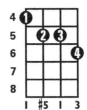

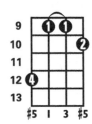

Esus2

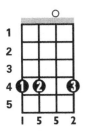

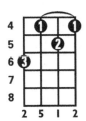

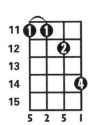

Esus4

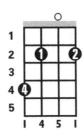

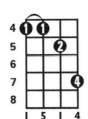

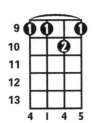

E7sus4

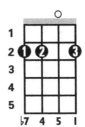

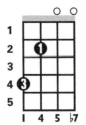

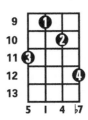

Em7-5

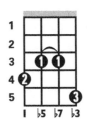

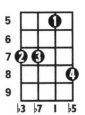

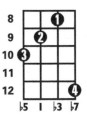

E Chords

Eadd9	Emadd9	E6add9	Em6add9

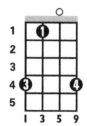 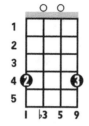 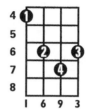 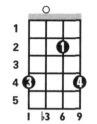

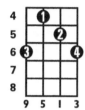 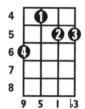 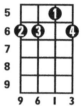 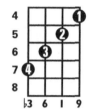

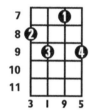 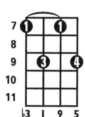 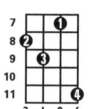 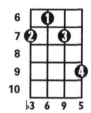

E7-5	E7+5	E7-9	E7+9

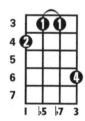 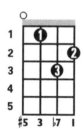 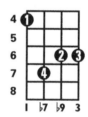 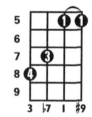

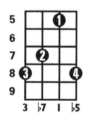 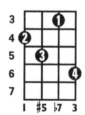 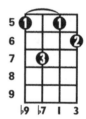 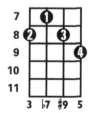

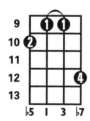 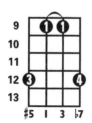 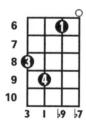 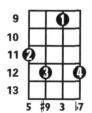

Em(maj7)

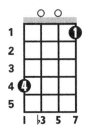

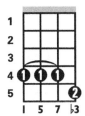

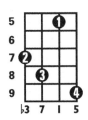

Emaj7-5

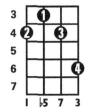

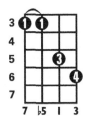

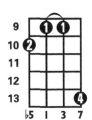

Emaj7+5

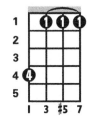

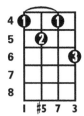

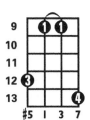

E9

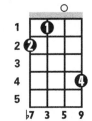

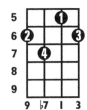

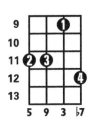

Em9

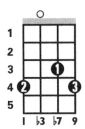

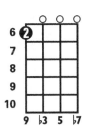

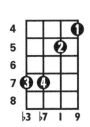

Emaj9

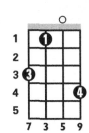

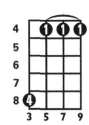

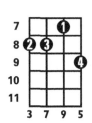

E11

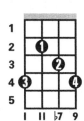

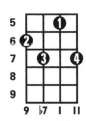

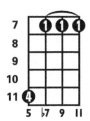

E13

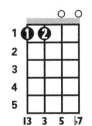

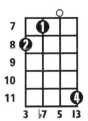

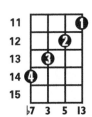

E Chords (Advanced)

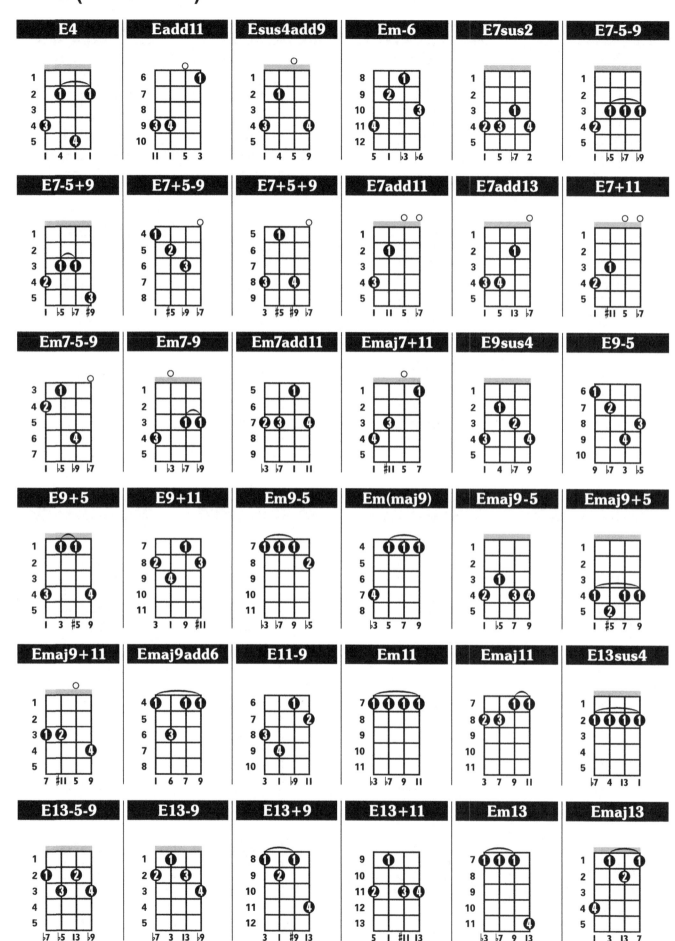

F Chords

F

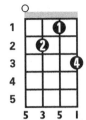

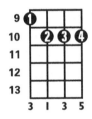

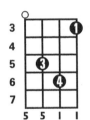

Fm

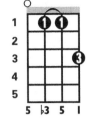

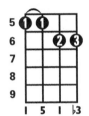

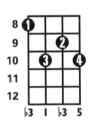

F7

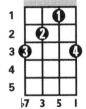

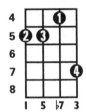

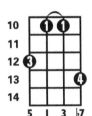

Fm7

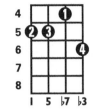

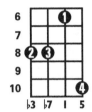

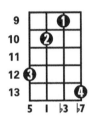

F5

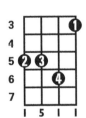

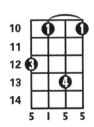

F6

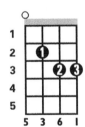

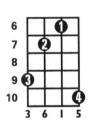

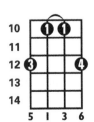

Fm6

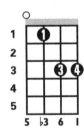

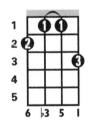

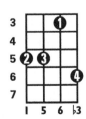

Fmaj7

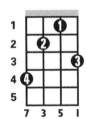

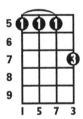

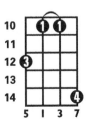

F Chords

F°
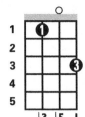
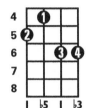
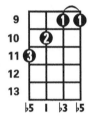

F°7
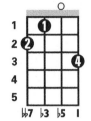
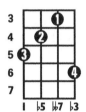
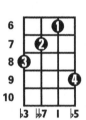

F-5
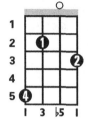
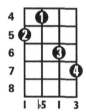
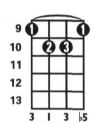

F+
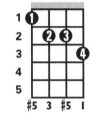
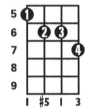
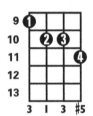

Fsus2
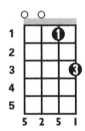
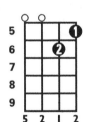
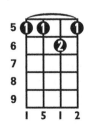

Fsus4
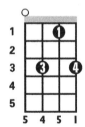
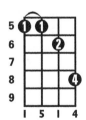
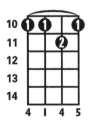

F7sus4
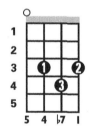
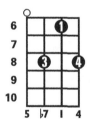
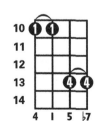

Fm7-5
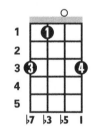
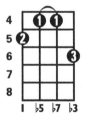
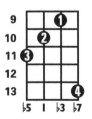

F Chords

Fadd9

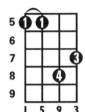

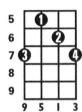

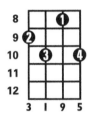

Fmadd9

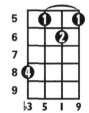

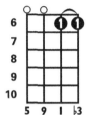

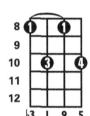

F6add9

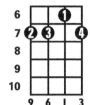

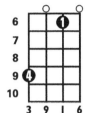

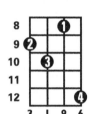

Fm6add9

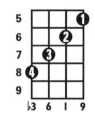

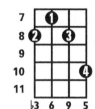

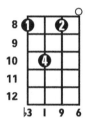

F7-5

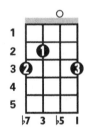

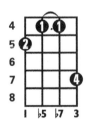

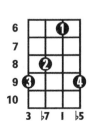

F7+5

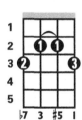

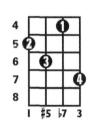

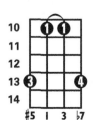

F7-9

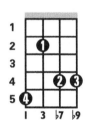

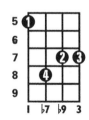

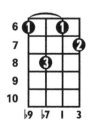

F7+9

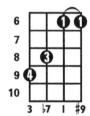

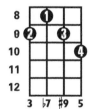

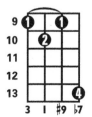

F Chords

Fm(maj7)
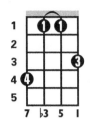
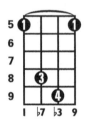

Fmaj7-5
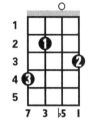
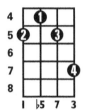
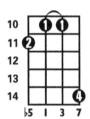

Fmaj7+5
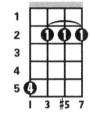
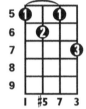
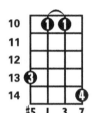

F9
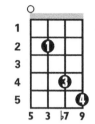
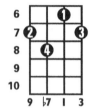
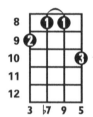

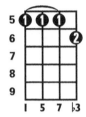
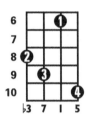

Fm9
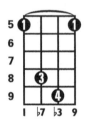
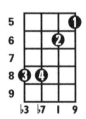
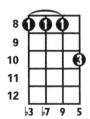

Fmaj9
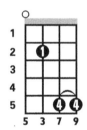
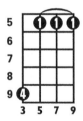
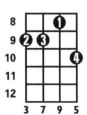

F11
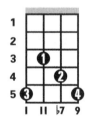
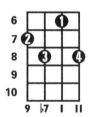
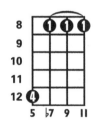

F13
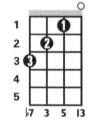
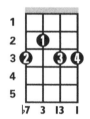
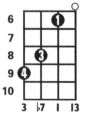

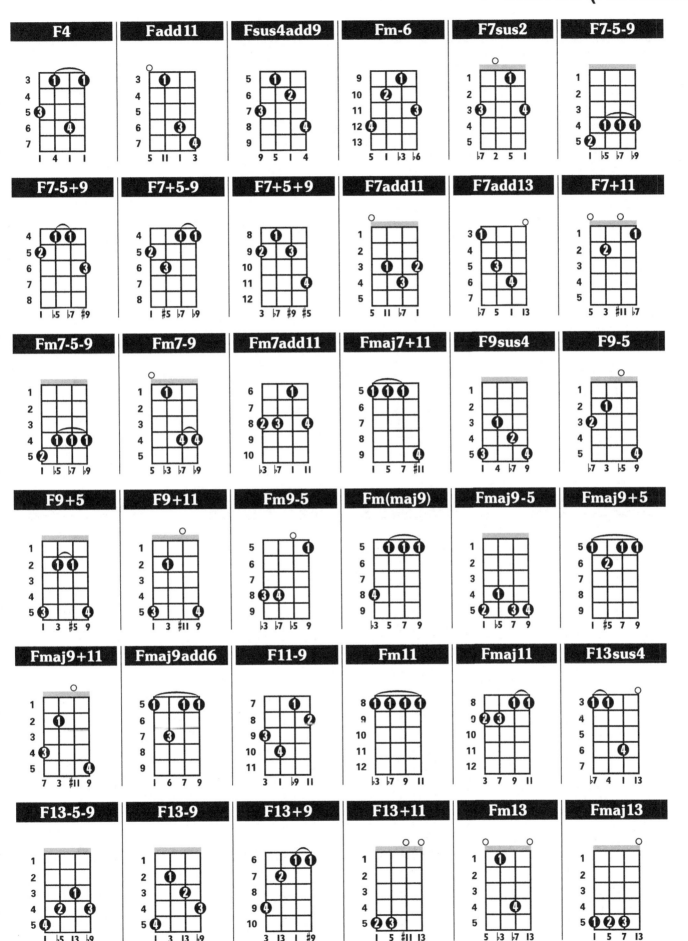

F# / G♭ Chords

F#	F#m	F#7	F#m7

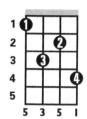 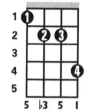 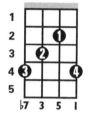 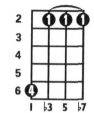

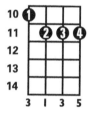 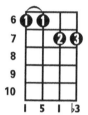 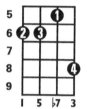 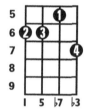

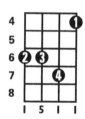 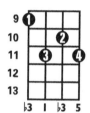 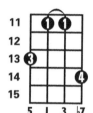 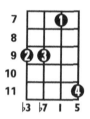

F#5	F#6	F#m6	F#maj7

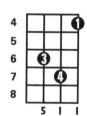 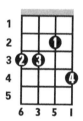 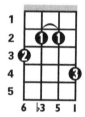 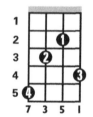

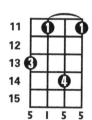 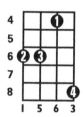 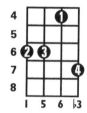 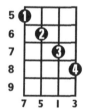

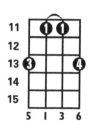 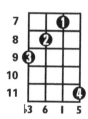 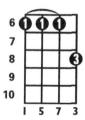

42

F#/ Gb Chords

F#°
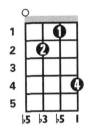
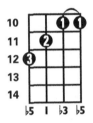
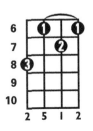

F#°7
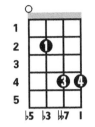
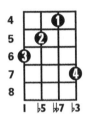
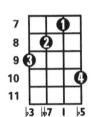

F#-5
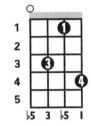
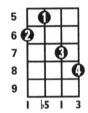
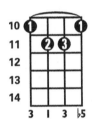

F#+
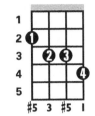
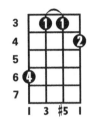
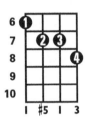

F#sus2
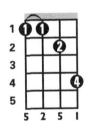
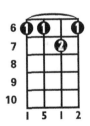

F#sus4
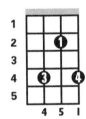
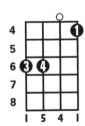
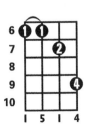

F#7sus4
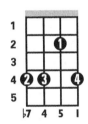
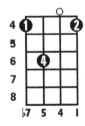
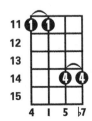

F#m7-5
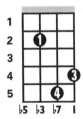
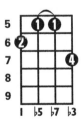
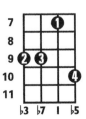

43

F♯/ G♭ Chords

F#add9

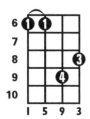

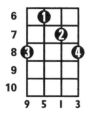

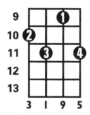

F#madd9

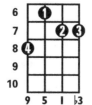

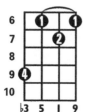

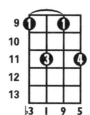

F#6add9

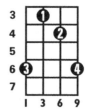

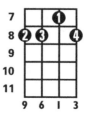

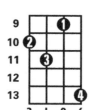

F#m6add9

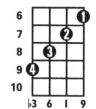

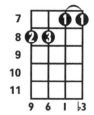

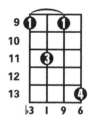

F#7-5

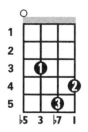

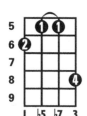

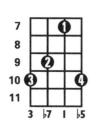

F#7+5

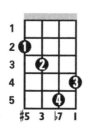

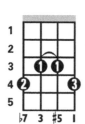

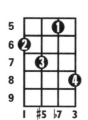

F#7-9

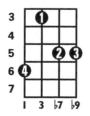

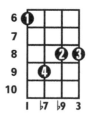

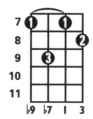

F#7+9

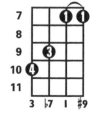

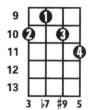

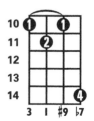

44

F#m(maj7)

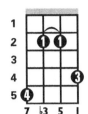

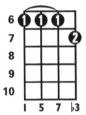

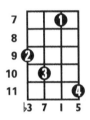

F#maj7-5

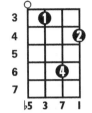

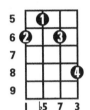

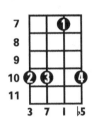

F#maj7+5

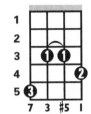

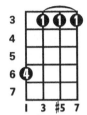

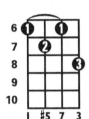

F#9

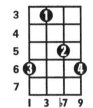

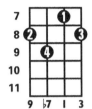

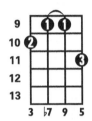

F#m9

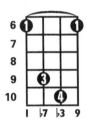

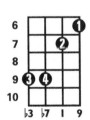

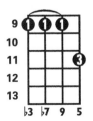

F#maj9

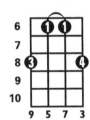

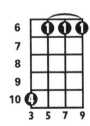

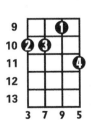

F#11

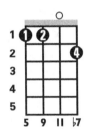

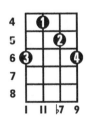

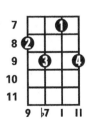

F#13

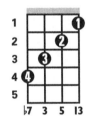

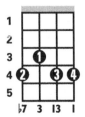

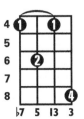

F♯ / G♭ Chords (Advanced)

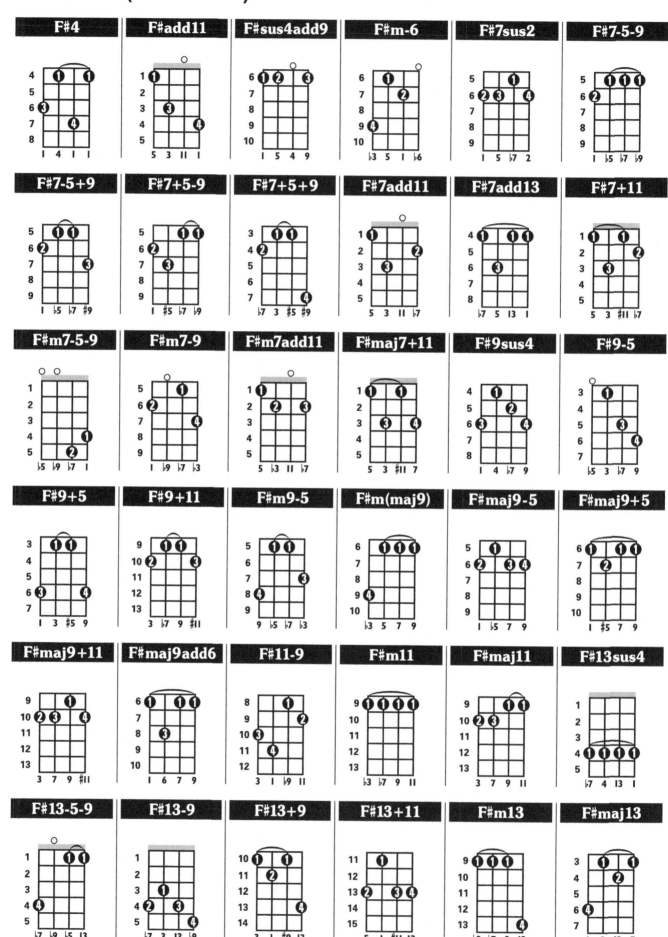

G
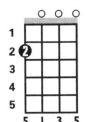
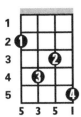
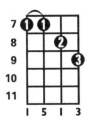

Gm
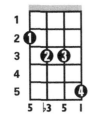
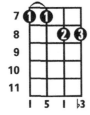
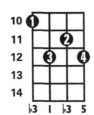

G7
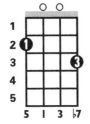
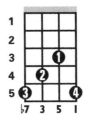
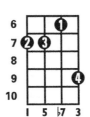

Gm7
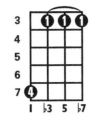
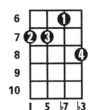
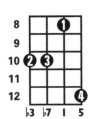

G5
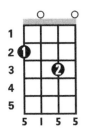
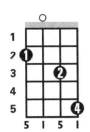
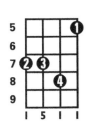

G6
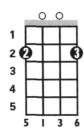
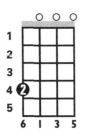
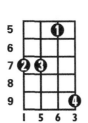

Gm6
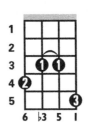
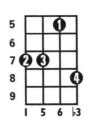
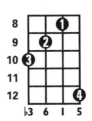

Gmaj7
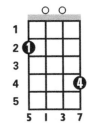
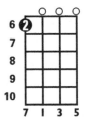
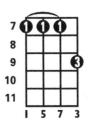

G Chords

Gº

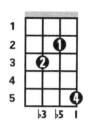

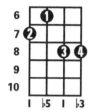

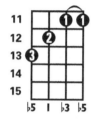

Gº7

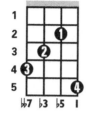

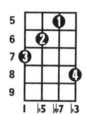

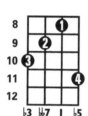

G-5

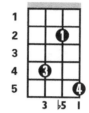

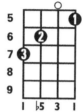

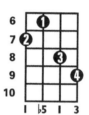

G+

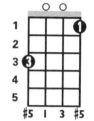

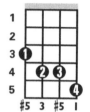

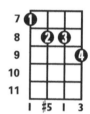

Gsus2

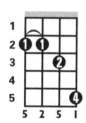

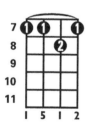

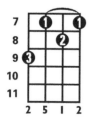

Gsus4

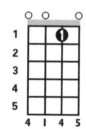

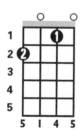

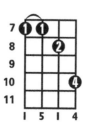

G7sus4

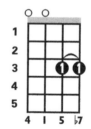

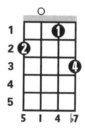

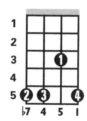

Gm7-5

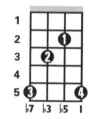

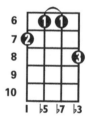

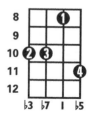

G Chords

Gadd9
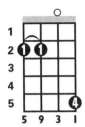
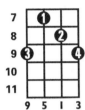
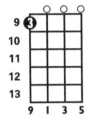

Gmadd9
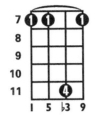
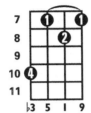
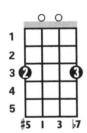

G6add9
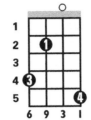
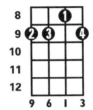
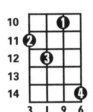

Gm6add9
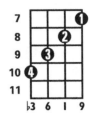
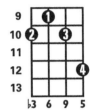
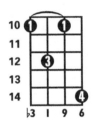

G7-5
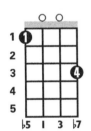
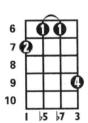
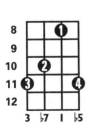

G7+5
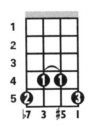
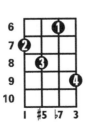

G7-9
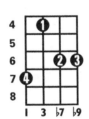
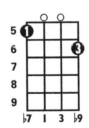
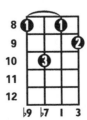

G7+9
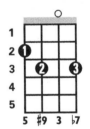
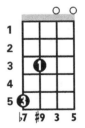
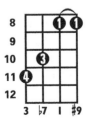

49

G Chords

Gm(maj7)
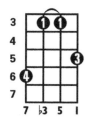
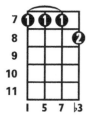
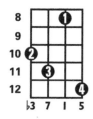

Gmaj7-5
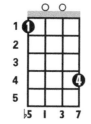
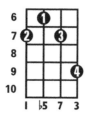
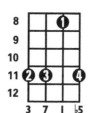

Gmaj7+5
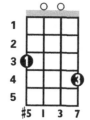
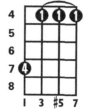
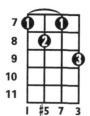

G9
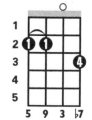
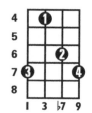
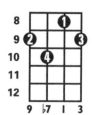

Gm9
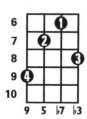
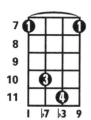
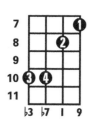

Gmaj9
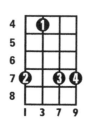
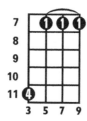
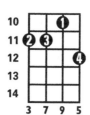

G11
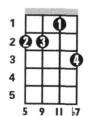
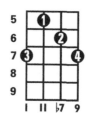
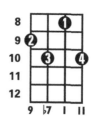

G13
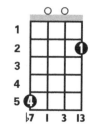
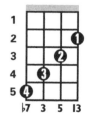
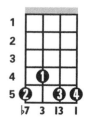

50

G Chords (Advanced)

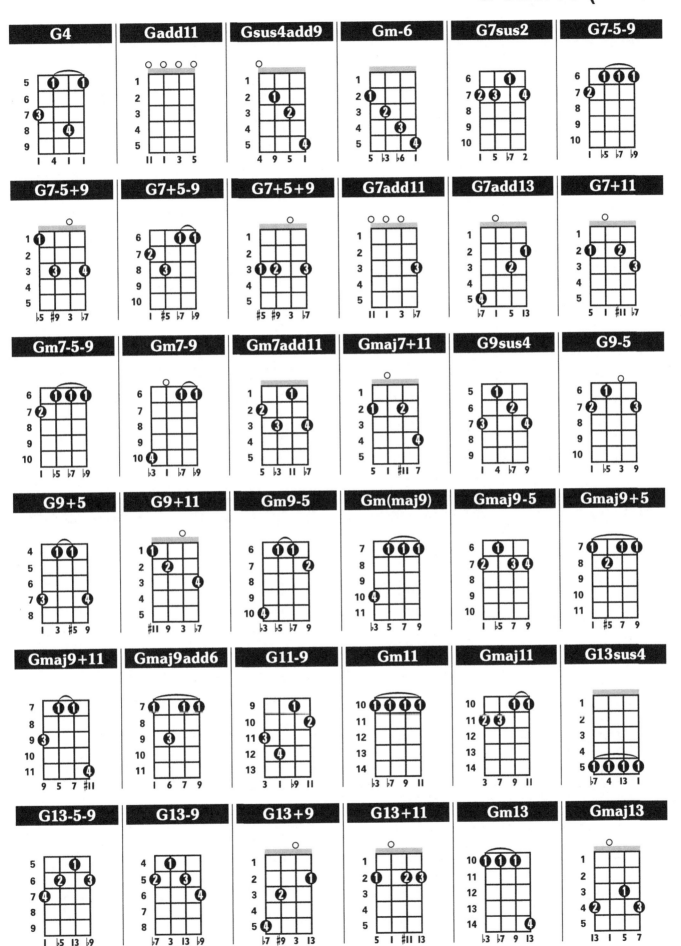

G# / A♭ Chords

A♭

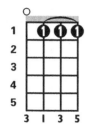

3 I 3 5

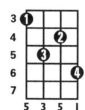

5 3 5 I

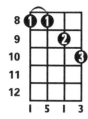

I 5 I 3

A♭m

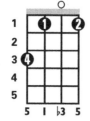

5 I ♭3 5

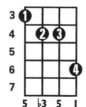

5 ♭3 5 I

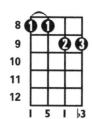

I 5 I ♭3

A♭7

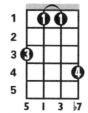

5 I 3 ♭7

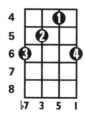

♭7 3 5 I

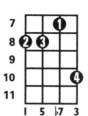

I 5 ♭7 3

A♭m7

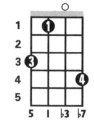

5 I ♭3 ♭7

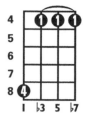

I ♭3 5 ♭7

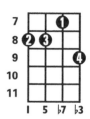

I 5 ♭7 ♭3

A♭5

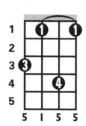

5 I 5 5

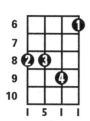

I 5 I I

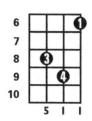

5 I I

A♭6

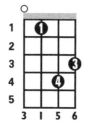

3 I 5 6

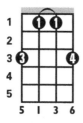

5 I 3 6

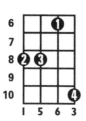

I 5 6 3

A♭m6

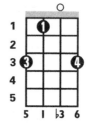

5 I ♭3 6

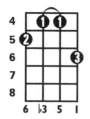

6 ♭3 5 I

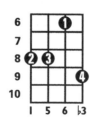

I 5 6 ♭3

A♭maj7

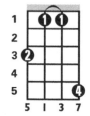

5 I 3 7

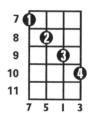

7 5 I 3

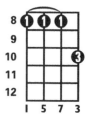

I 5 7 3

52

A♭°

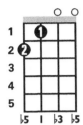

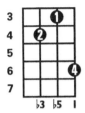

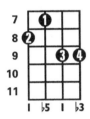

A♭°7

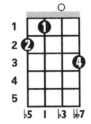

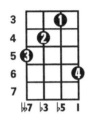

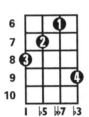

A♭-5

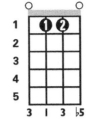

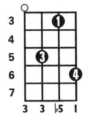

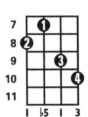

A♭+

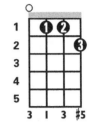

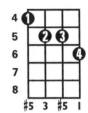

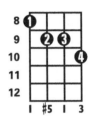

A♭sus2

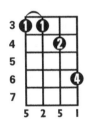

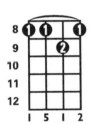

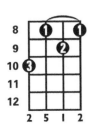

A♭sus4

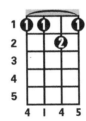

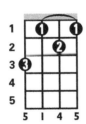

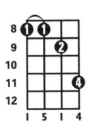

A♭7sus4

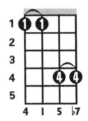

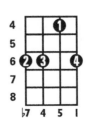

A♭m7-5

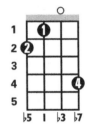

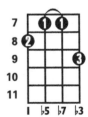

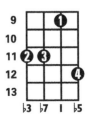

G# / A♭ Chords

A♭add9

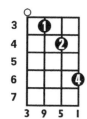

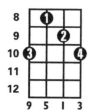

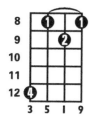

A♭madd9

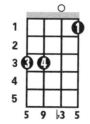

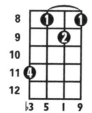

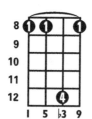

A♭6add9

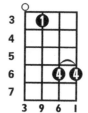

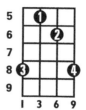

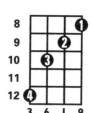

A♭m6add9

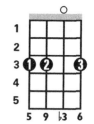

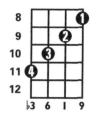

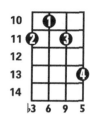

A♭7-5

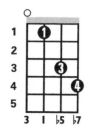

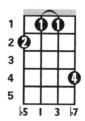

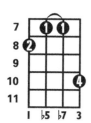

A♭7+5

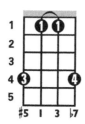

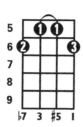

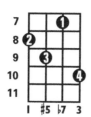

A♭7-9

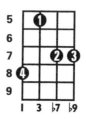

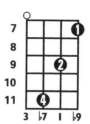

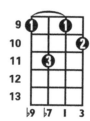

A♭7+9

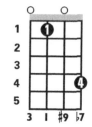

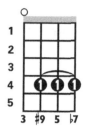

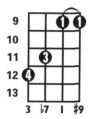

54

A♭m(maj7)
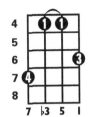
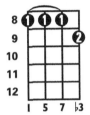
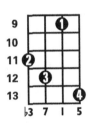

A♭maj7-5
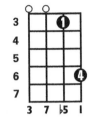
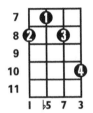
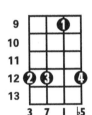

A♭maj7+5
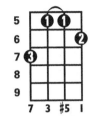
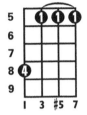
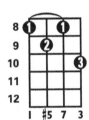

A♭9
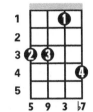
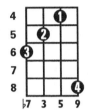

A♭m9
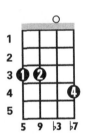
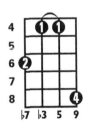
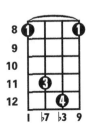

A♭maj9
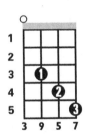
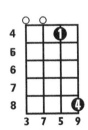
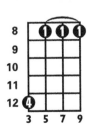

A♭11
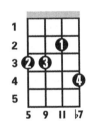
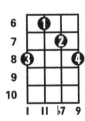
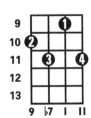

A♭13
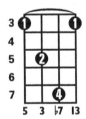
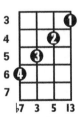
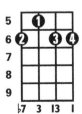

G# / A♭ Chords (Advanced)

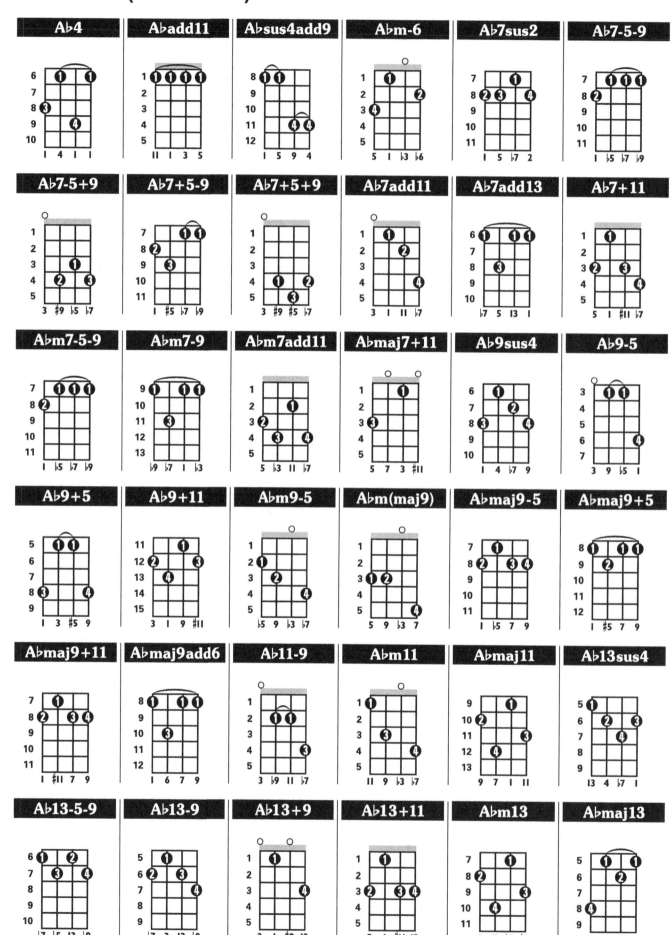

A Chords

A
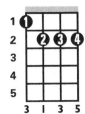
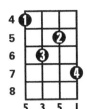
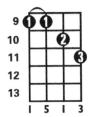

Am
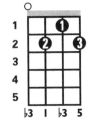
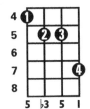
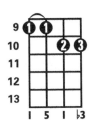

A7
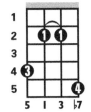
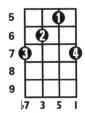
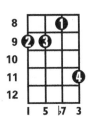

Am7
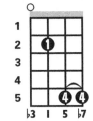
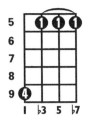
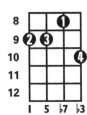

A5
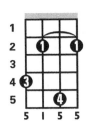
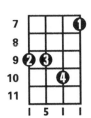
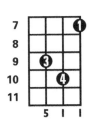

A6
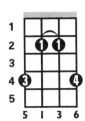
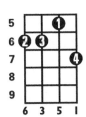
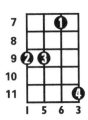

Am6
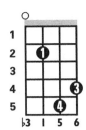
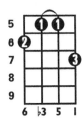
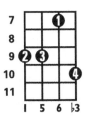

Amaj7
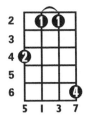
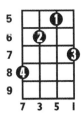
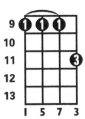

A Chords

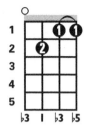
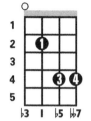
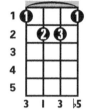
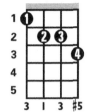
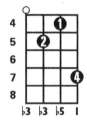
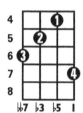
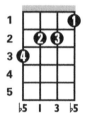
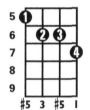
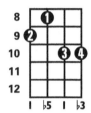
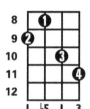
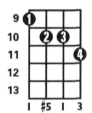
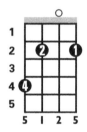
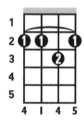
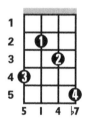
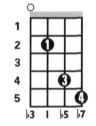
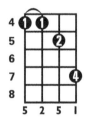
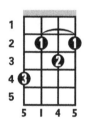
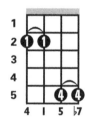
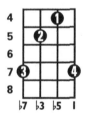
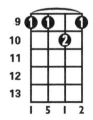
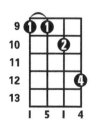
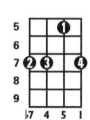
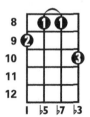

A Chords

Aadd9

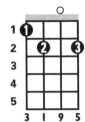

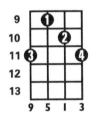

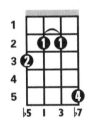

Amadd9

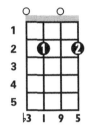

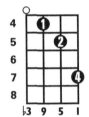

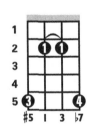

A6add9

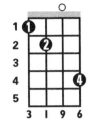

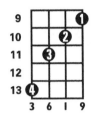

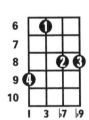

Am6add9

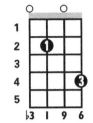

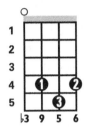

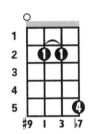

A7-5

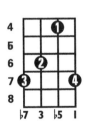

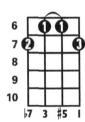

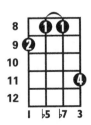

A7+5

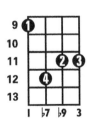

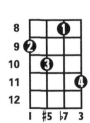

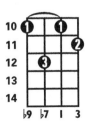

A7-9

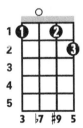

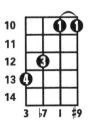

A7+9

59

A Chords

Am(maj7)

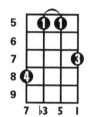

7 ♭3 5 I

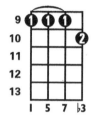

I 5 7 ♭3

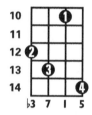

♭3 7 I 5

Amaj7-5

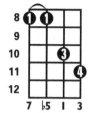

7 ♭5 I 3

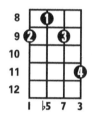

I ♭5 7 3

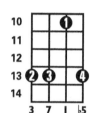

3 7 I ♭5

Amaj7+5

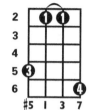

#5 I 3 7

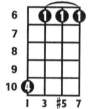

I 3 #5 7

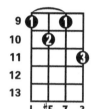

I #5 7 3

A9

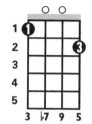

3 ♭7 9 5

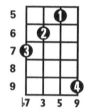

♭7 3 5 9

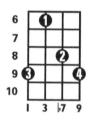

I 3 ♭7 9

Am9

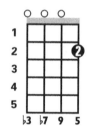

♭3 ♭7 9 5

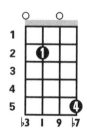

♭3 I 9 ♭7

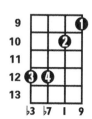

♭3 ♭7 I 9

Amaj9

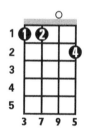

3 7 9 5

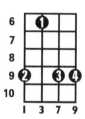

I 3 7 9

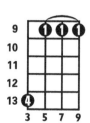

3 5 7 9

A11

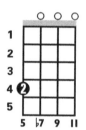

5 ♭7 9 11

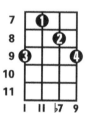

I 11 ♭7 9

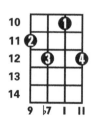

9 ♭7 I 11

A13

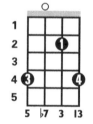

5 ♭7 3 13

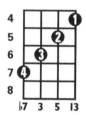

♭7 3 5 13

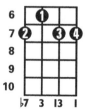

♭7 3 13 I

60

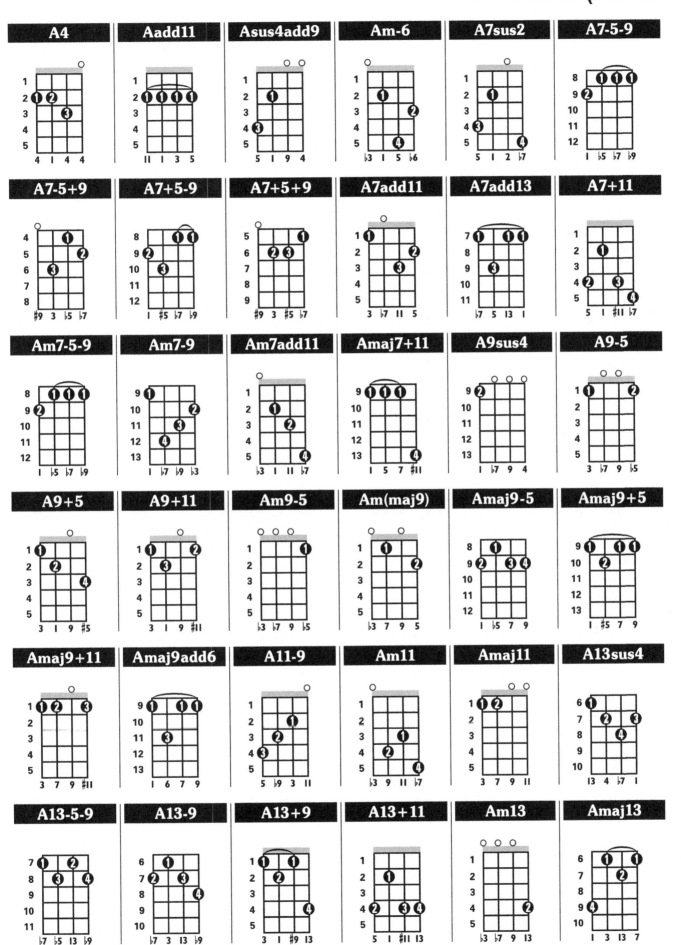

A# / B♭ Chords

B♭	B♭m	B♭7	B♭m7

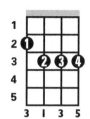
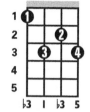
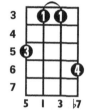
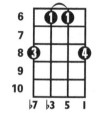

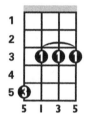
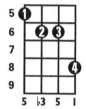
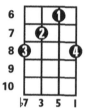
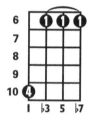

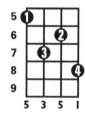
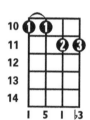
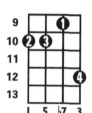
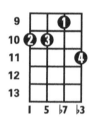

B♭5	B♭6	B♭m6	B♭maj7

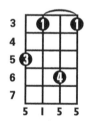
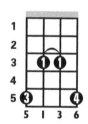
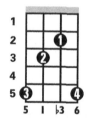
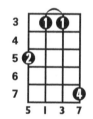

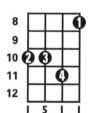
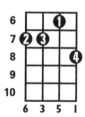
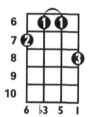
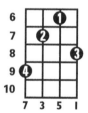

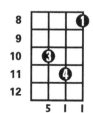
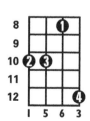
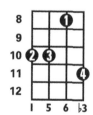
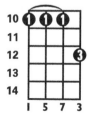

B♭°

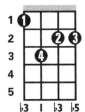

B♭°7

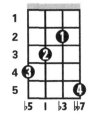

B♭-5

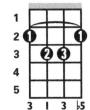

B♭+

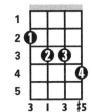

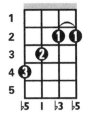

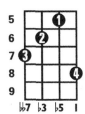

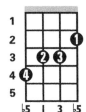

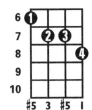

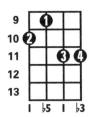

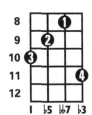

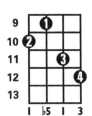

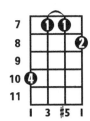

B♭sus2

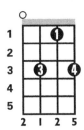

B♭sus4

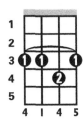

B♭7sus4

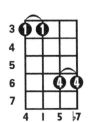

B♭m7-5

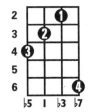

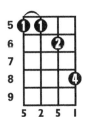

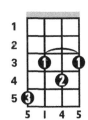

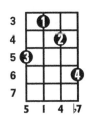

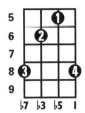

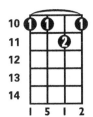

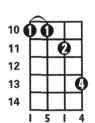

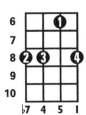

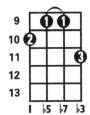

A#/B♭ Chords

B♭add9
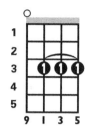

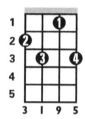

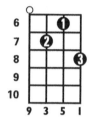

B♭madd9
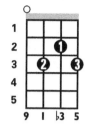

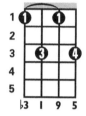

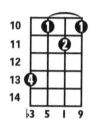

B♭6add9
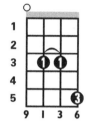

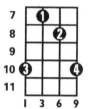

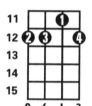

B♭m6add9
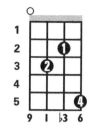

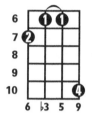

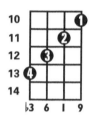

B♭7-5
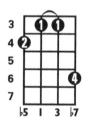

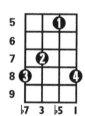

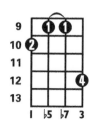

B♭7+5
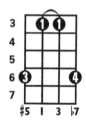

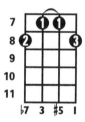

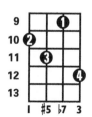

B♭7-9
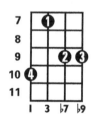

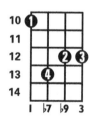

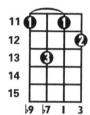

B♭7+9
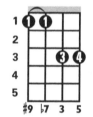

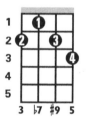

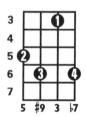

B♭m(maj7)

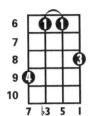

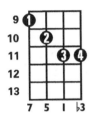

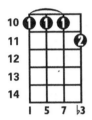

B♭maj7-5

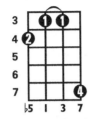

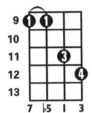

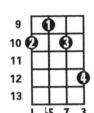

B♭maj7+5

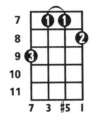

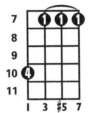

B♭9

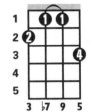

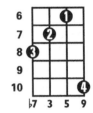

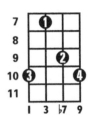

B♭m9

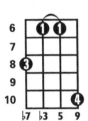

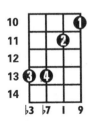

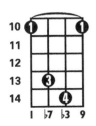

B♭maj9

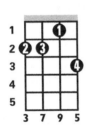

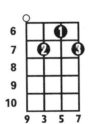

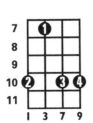

B♭11

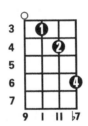

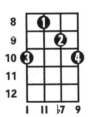

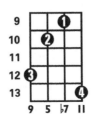

B♭13

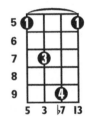

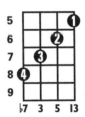

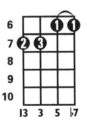

A# / B♭ Chords (Advanced)

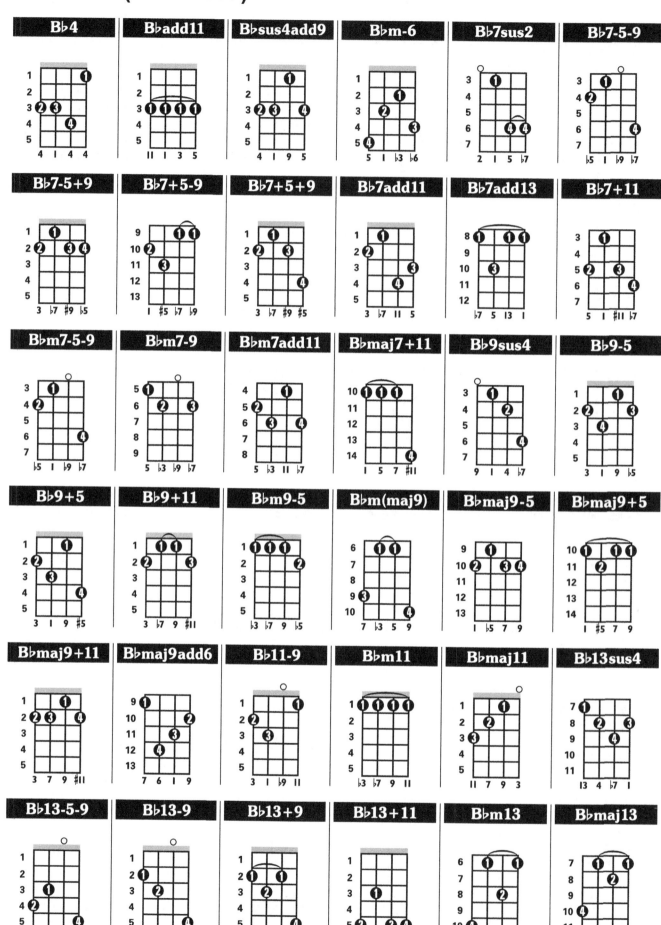

B Chords

B

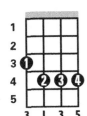
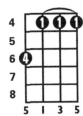
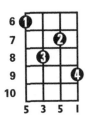

Bm

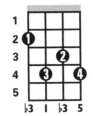
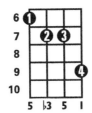
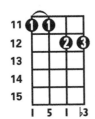

B7

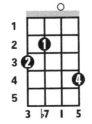
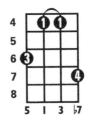
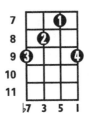

Bm7

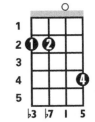
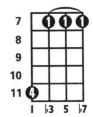
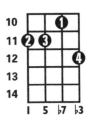

B5

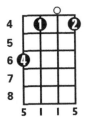
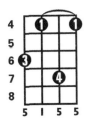
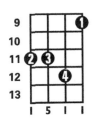

B6

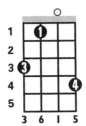
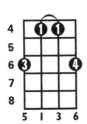

Bm6

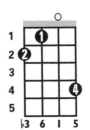
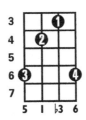
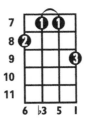

Bmaj7

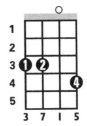
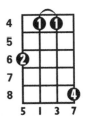
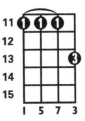

B Chords

B°
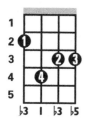
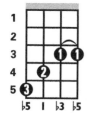
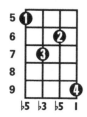

B°7
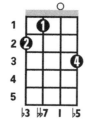
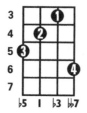
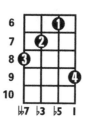

B-5
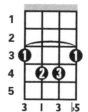
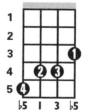
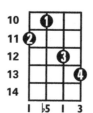

B+
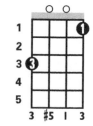
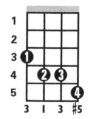
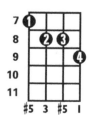

Bsus2
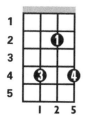
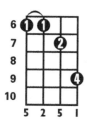
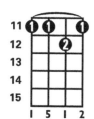

Bsus4
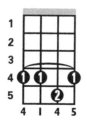
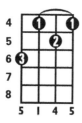
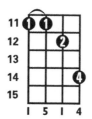

B7sus4
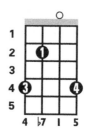
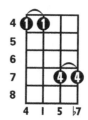
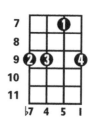

Bm7-5
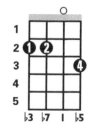
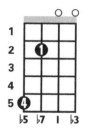
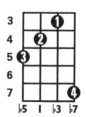

B Chords

Badd9

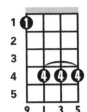

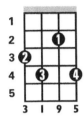

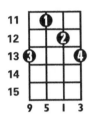

Bmadd9

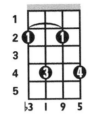

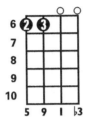

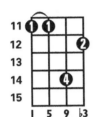

B6add9

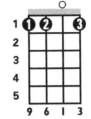

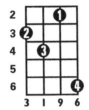

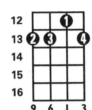

Bm6add9

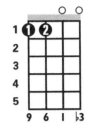

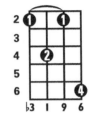

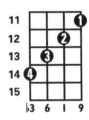

B7-5

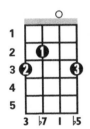

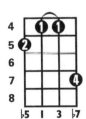

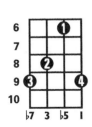

B7+5

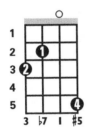

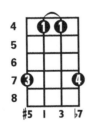

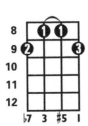

B7-9

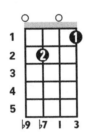

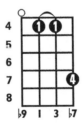

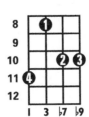

B7+9

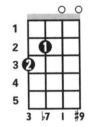

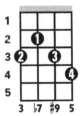

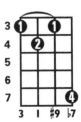

B Chords

Bm(maj7)
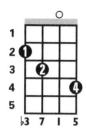
♭3 7 1 5

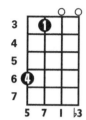
5 7 1 ♭3

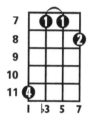
1 ♭3 5 7

Bmaj7-5
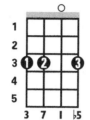
3 7 1 ♭5

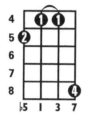
♭5 1 3 7

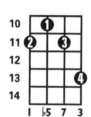
1 ♭5 7 3

Bmaj7+5
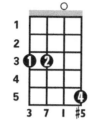
3 7 1 #5

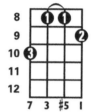
7 3 #5 1

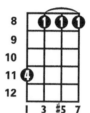
1 3 #5 7

B9
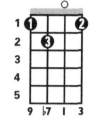
9 ♭7 1 3

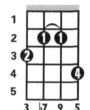
3 ♭7 9 5

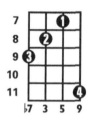
♭7 3 5 9

Bm9
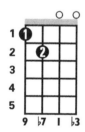
9 ♭7 1 ♭3

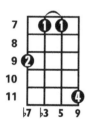
♭7 ♭3 5 9

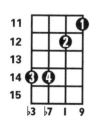
♭3 ♭7 1 9

Bmaj9
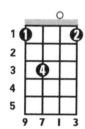
9 7 1 3

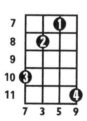
7 3 5 9

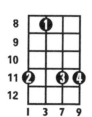
1 3 7 9

B11
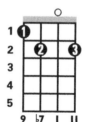
9 ♭7 1 11

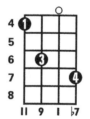
11 9 1 ♭7

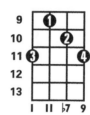
1 11 ♭7 9

B13
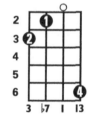
3 ♭7 1 13

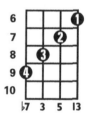
♭7 3 5 13

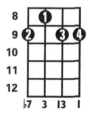
♭7 3 13 1

B Chords (Advanced)

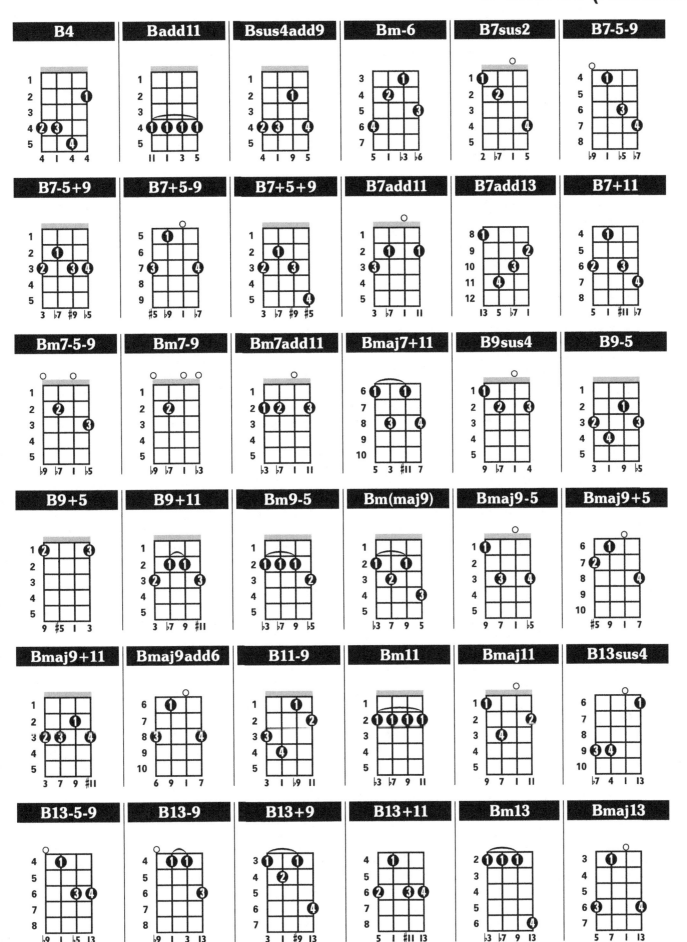

Major Slash Chords

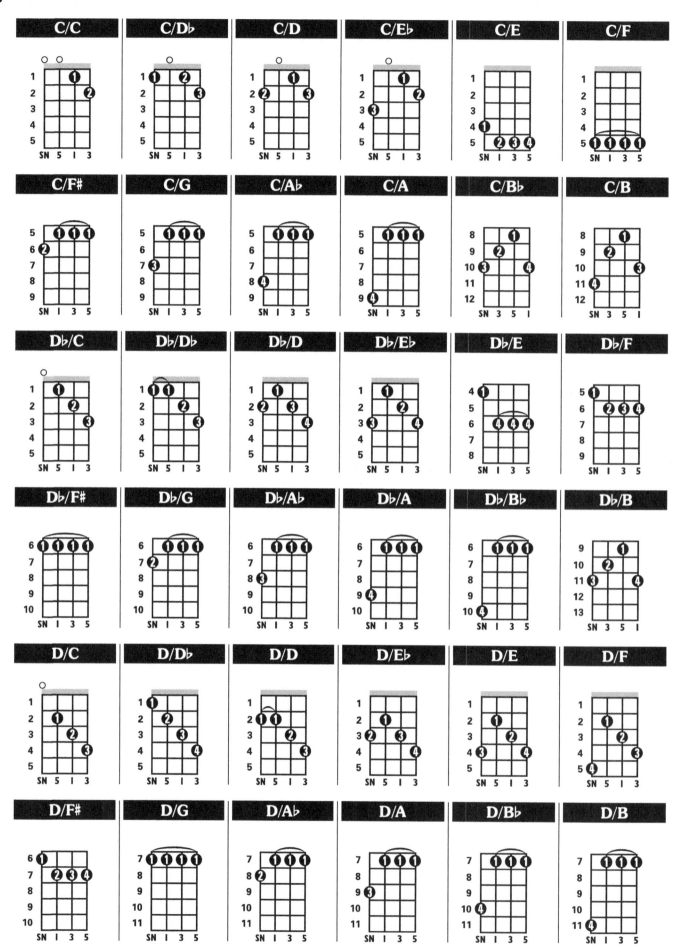

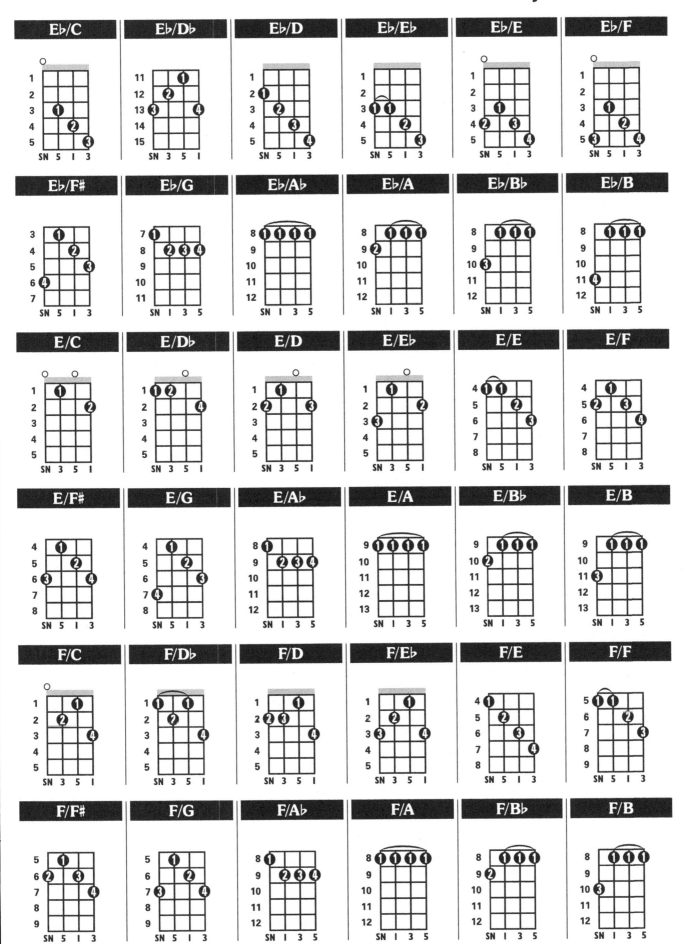

Major Slash Chords

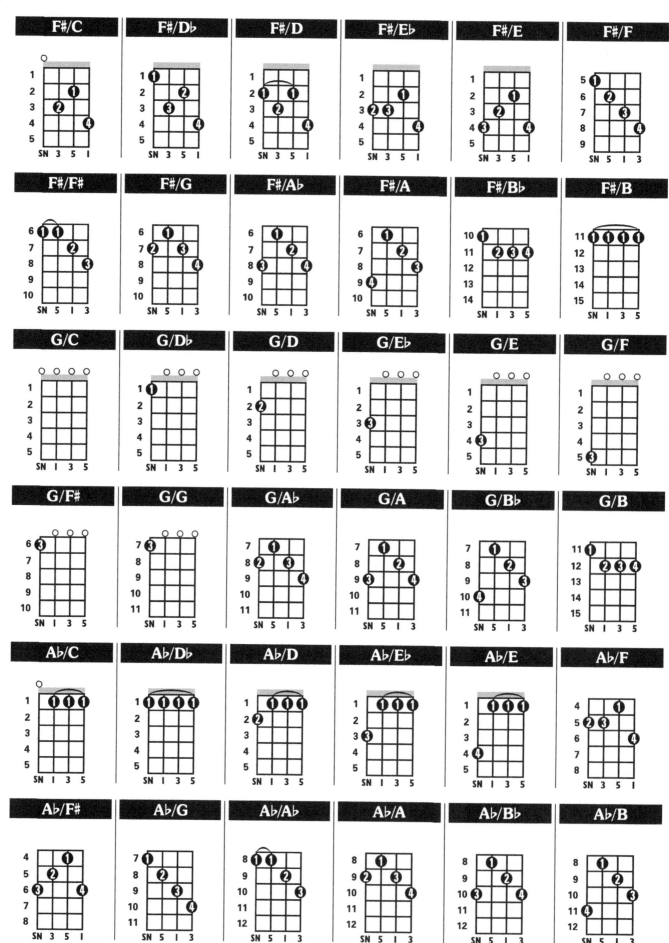

Major Slash Chords

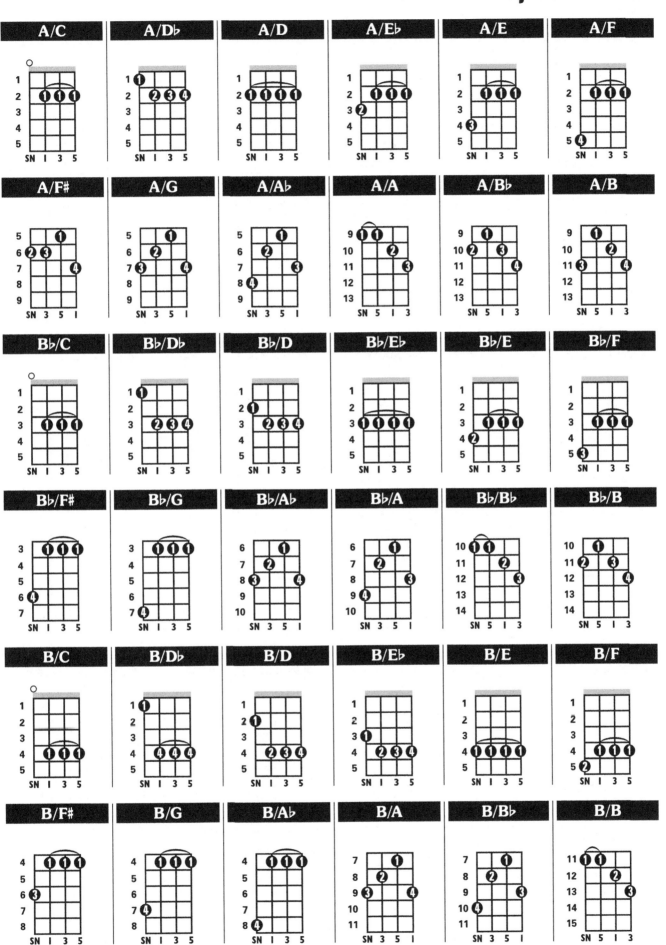

A Selection of Moveable Chord Shapes

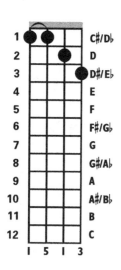
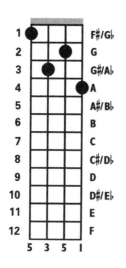
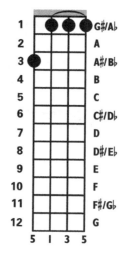
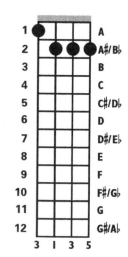

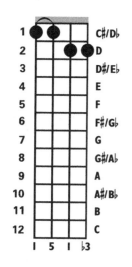
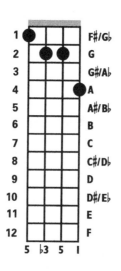
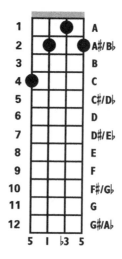
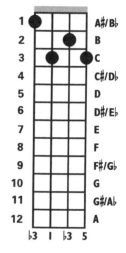

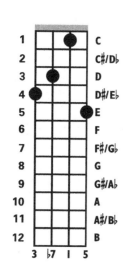
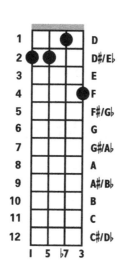
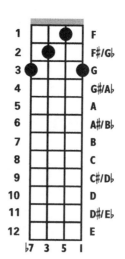
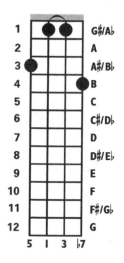

A Selection of Moveable Chord Shapes

Minor Seventh
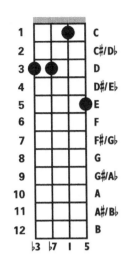

Minor Seventh
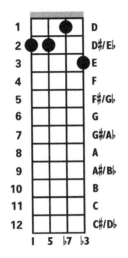

Minor Seventh
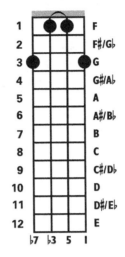

Minor Seventh
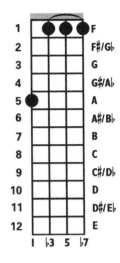

Sixth
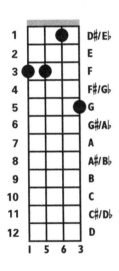

Sixth
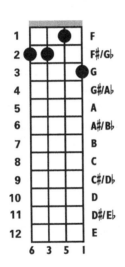

Sixth
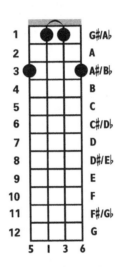

Sixth
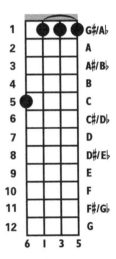

Minor Sixth
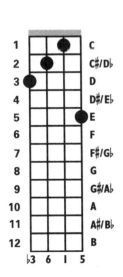

Minor Sixth
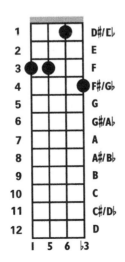

Minor Sixth
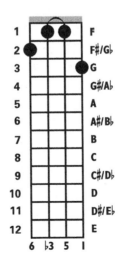

Minor Sixth
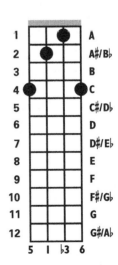

A Selection of Moveable Chord Shapes

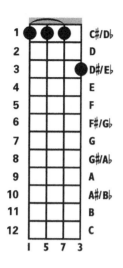

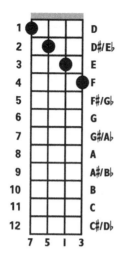

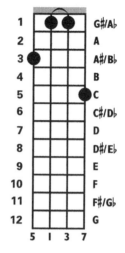

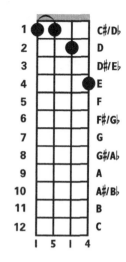

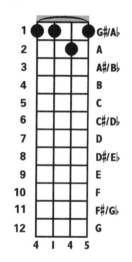

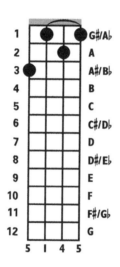

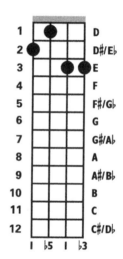

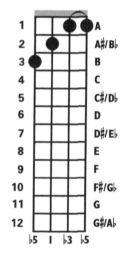

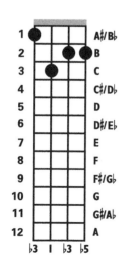

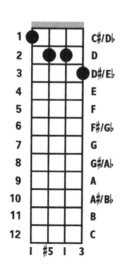

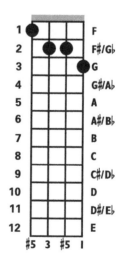

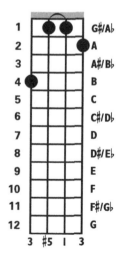

A Selection of Moveable Chord Shapes

Diminished Seventh
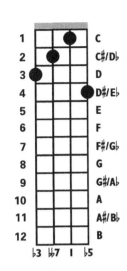

Diminished Seventh
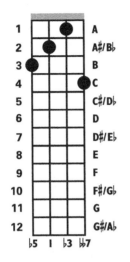

Fifth
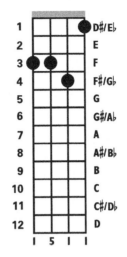

Fifth
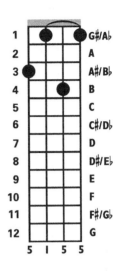

Seventh Suspended
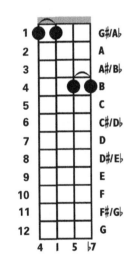

Added Ninth
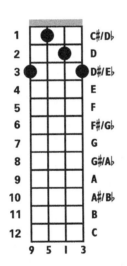

Added Ninth
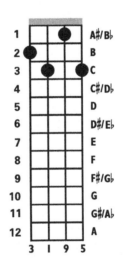

Ninth
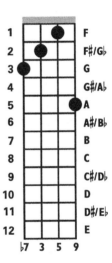

Minor Ninth
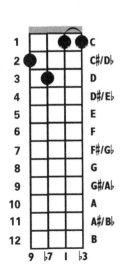

Major Ninth
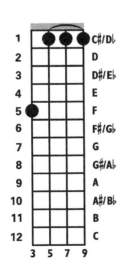

Eleventh
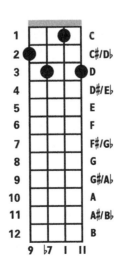

Thirteenth
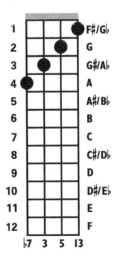

79

BANJO FAMILY FACTFILE

A Scale or Travel Banjo
A shorter scale 5-string banjo tuned a whole tone above the G banjo.

Banjeaurine, Banjorine or Pony Banjo
A little 5-string banjo built by the American maker, SS Stewart and used primarily as a lead instrument in banjo, mandolin and guitar orchestras. After a few years, the banjeaurine was replaced by the similarly named banjolin. The modern version, the Pony, is tuned a fourth higher than a regular 5-string in open C.

Banjo - A Brief History
Pinpointing the true origins of the banjo is a difficult task, but most historians believe the instrument we know today can be traced back to Africa and brought to America and the Caribbean region during the darkest days of the slave trade. Although its African lineage is more than conjecture, it's also likely that banjo-like instruments were transplanted into African culture by way of Middle Eastern migrants. Western references to the banjo were appearing as early as the seventeenth century, with a large number of variants making their individual marks along this twisting musical road throughout the past three or four centuries.

In both eighteenth century America and Britain, the popularity of the instrument led to all manner of configurations appearing, including five, six, seven and nine string versions. Today, there are fewer variants being made, but the banjo is as firmly entrenched in the public's musical consciousness as the guitar or mandolin. Of all the fretted instruments in today's varied musical landscape, the plunk of the banjo is arguably the most instantly recognisable of them all.

Banjola
A combination of a 5-string banjo neck and a celtic mandolin or mandola body. This is an ideal instrument for 5-string players wishing to explore new tonal qualities without having to learn a different tuning/fingering arrangement. The sound is a lot mellower and less plunky than a standard 5-string. The tuning, as you'd imagine, can be anything from bluegrass open G to double C.

Banjolele or Banjo-Ukulele
A popular instrument with its heyday in the 20's and 30's, the banjolele or banjo-uke is basically a ukulele in a short scaled banjo's body. These entertaining instruments can be tuned GCEA or ADF#B. The banjolele was popularized in the U.K. by comedian George Formby, where the instrument was mistakenly referred to at the time as a ukulele. The name banjolele was originally created by the Keech Brothers, Alvin and Kel. Notable players include Roy Smeck, Arthur Godfrey, Billy Scott and Tessie O'Shea.

Banjolin
Very similar to the mandolin banjo, but with four single strings instead of 4 double courses of strings. These generally have open backs, but occasionally some of them are fitted out with resonators. The banjolin is tuned GDAE, like a mandolin.

Bass and Contrabass Banjo
The original bass banjos were around the size of a typical double bass, if not a little wider to accommodate the oversized body and head. Over the years these have been scaled down somewhat and today's examples are around the size of an acoustic bass guitar. A modern example is the model produced by the banjo company, Gold Tone. The contrabass was an even larger model featuring CGDA or cello-style tuning.

Cello Banjo
A large sized 5-string variant played in the upright position. You won't see one of these in your average music shop.

Clawhammer or Claw-hammer Banjo
Another name for the open-back banjo, so-called because of the clawhammer technique employed on the instrument. Where it differs from frailing is that clawhammer techniques don't just pick the 5th drone string. The player can also use the thumb to pick out a melody - a method called drop thumb or double thumbing. In some musical circles, the dinstinction between clawhammer and frailing is fairly blured. Well known clawhammer players include: Bob Carlin, Dwight Diller, Dan Levenson, Brad Leftwich, and Abigail Washburn.

Cümbüs
A Turkish instrument that comes in a variety of configurations, both with and without frets. The tunings vary according to the type, with guitar and mandolin versions standing alongside more traditional oud and saz stringing arrangements. The cümbüs (pronounced Joom-bush) was invented in the 1930's by Zeynel Abidin Cümbüs, a Turkish instrument seller with Macedonian roots. The instrument remained popular for several decades until its appeal waned in 1960's Turkey. The traditional banjo rose in popularity and the cümbüs appeared to be on the way out. But by chance, American multi-instrumentalist, David Lindley discovered one in a California music store and started using it on a regular basis. So, mainly thanks to Lindley and a few others, this unique cousin of the banjo remains a popular minority instrument to this day.

Electric Banjo
Not to be outdone by other fretted instruments, the banjo has also received the circuitry treatment. One of the best known models currently available is the Crossfire played by 5-string luminaries such as Bela Fleck and Tony Trishka. The advantage of the electric model over the much more predominant acoustics is the lack of feedback for stage work. But, arguably, the acoustic banjo will always have the edge over it's electric counterpart in terms of tone and feel.

Frailing Banjo
An alternative name for the open-back 5-string banjo. The technique of frailing involves striking the 5th drone string in a downward motion after each strum.

Fretless Banjo
Early commercial banjos started out as fretless instruments in the mid-half of the 1800's. They often featured six or seven strings - a configuration that was common until the 5-string gained prominence.

5-String or G Banjo
When you think of the 5-string or G banjo, most aficionados would immediately think of bluegrass maestro Earl Scruggs. The Scruggs three finger style of playing undoubtedly blazed a trail in bluegrass music, but the origins of the actual instrument go back to much earlier times. A minstrel musician called Joel Walker Sweeney has often been credited with the invention of the 5th string drone, but there is evidence in the form of an earlier painting called The Old Plantation, that the drone string was already being utilised by African American slaves.

Two main types of 5-string remain popular today. Firstly, the earlier open-back style which tends to be used for clawhammer or frailing styles and secondly, the closed-back resonator models favoured by bluegrass players like Scruggs and Trishka. As the name implies the resonator models generate a greater volume because of the way the body chamber is designed.

The most popular tuning for the 5-string is probably open Open G or Bluegrass (gDGBD) and Standard C (gCGBD). But like the guitar, a myriad of variations have sprung up over the years, with some of the most popular being: Open C (gCGCE), Double C for clawhammer styles (gCGCD), *Open D* (a or f#DF#AD), *G modal* or *Sawmill* (also called *Mountain Minor*) tuning (gDGCD) and *G Minor* (gDGB D).

Famous players include: *Earl Scruggs, Tony Trishka, Béla Fleck, Ralph Stanley, Pete Seeger, Dwight Diller, Grandpa Jones, David "Stringbean" Akeman, Tony Furtado, Uncle Dave Macon* and *Doug Dillard*.

Mandolin Banjo
Basically a mandolin in a banjo's body. These were particularly popular during the early part of the last century. Like a regular mandolin, the mandolin banjo is tuned GDAE.

Piccolo Banjo
A small 5-string banjo pitched an octave higher than a standard G banjo. These little instruments have long since gone out of fashion, except for the few that occasionally turn up or are specially commissioned and built by banjo luthiers.

Plectrum Banjo
The plectrum banjo, as its title implies, should be played with a pick or plectrum. This long scale member of the banjo family should have 22 frets and is usually tuned CGBD. The plectrum is generally considered to be more of a melody chord playing instrument and was particularly popular during the Dixieland era. The tuning arrangement tends to give the plectrum more of a mellow feeling with respect to chord playing. An alternative tuning for the plectrum banjo is referred to as *guitar tuning* because it mirrors the first four strings of a guitar (i.e. DGBE low to high).

Seeger Banjo
An especially long scale open back 5-string which Pete Seeger commissioned to accommodate his vocal range. The Seeger banjo features an additional three frets before the fifth drone string comes into play and a scale of 32 inches (or 815mm), encompassing 25 frets.

6-String Guitar Banjo
Unfairly, the guitar banjo is looked on as something of a novelty instrument for guitarists who have little wish to put the hours in to learn to play the real thing. This is unfortunate as this variant is very much an instrument in its own right, with all the versatility of the six courses thrown in. Most players tend to use standard guitar tuning, but other configurations such as DADGAD or Drop D are just as valid. Predictably, as night follows day, 12-string versions of the guitar banjo have also appeared over the years. The sound is probably best described as *jingle-jangle-plunk!* The most famous exponent on the guitar banjo was probably the great jazz banjoist, *Johnny St. Cyr.* Other notable players include: *Danny Barker, Papa Charlie Jackson* and *Clancy Hayes*.

Tango Banjo
An early version of the tenor, named after the popular South American dance that was all the rage at the beginning of the 20th Century.. The tango features a shorter neck than today's tenors and only 15 frets.

Tenor Banjo
In banjo terms, the tenor is a relatively new instrument, first appearing in 1915. Traditionally, the tenor has between 17 and 19 frets as opposed to it's close relatives, the 5-string and plectrum models with 22 or over. Standard or Jazz tuning is CGDA, just like the mandola or viola. This is based on a progression of fifths where the next string is the equilavent of 7 frets up the fingerboard.

The original Irish banjos were long scaled instruments like the 5-string or plectrum models, bearing little resemblance to today's Irish tenors which are identical in every way to the standard tenor mentioned above (although some do have a shorter scale). The major difference between the two is the Irish tenor features a much lower tuning (GDAE), which is a forth down from standard tuning. This is basically the same as an octave mandolin (or octave mandola in the UK, Ireland and Europe). Famous players include: *Eddie Peabody, Roy Smeck, Elmer Snowden, Harry Reser, Perry Bechtel, Barney McKenna* and *Gerry O'Connor*.

Zither Banjo
The zither banjo had its heyday at the end of the nineteenth century and generally featured a wooden resonating chamber and an unusual 5th string mechanism. A metal tube was set into the neck underneath the fretboard and the 5th string was fed through the tube at the fifth fret, to appear at the appropriate tuner on the headstock. Another unique physical charactistic is the addition of a sixth tuner purely for decorative purposes. This was included to give a symmetrical appearance to the headstock (i.e. three tuners on each side). The head diameter was generally between 180-230mm (or 7 to 9 inches) where it rested on a cast metal body/wooden hoop arrangement, which in turn formed a convex-shaped back.

BANJO TUNINGS

The following list of banjo tunings includes a selection of some popular standards as well as some personal favourites. Some players stick with the same two ot three tunings all their lives, but others enjoy experimenting with new set-ups, but whichever you decide to do, have fun with this versatile family of instruments!

5-String Banjo

Open G *or* Bluegrass	gDGBD
Standard C	gCGBD
Open C	gCGCE
Open D	aDF#AD
Open D or *Rubin* Tuning	f#DF#AD
Double C	gCGCD
G Modal, Sawmill *or* Mountain Minor	gDGB D
G Minor	gDGB D
Moonshine	gDGAD
Dropped C	gCGBD
Guitar Tuning	gCGBD
D Minor	aDFAD
Seeger Banjo	gBEG#B
A-Scale Banjo Bluegrass Tuning	aEAC#E

Tenor Banjo

Standard *or* Jazz	CGDA
Irish	GDAE
Chicago	DGBE
D Tuning	D A E B
Eddie Freeman Special (EFS)	CGDA
High C (the C is raised an octave)	CGDA
High G (the G is raised an octave)	GDAE
Open D or DADA	DADA
Open C	CG
Bouzouki	DGBD
Modal *or* Bouzouki Tuning	DGAD

Plectrum Banjo

Standard	CGBD
Open G	DGBD
Chicago	DGBE
Eddie Freeman Special (EFS)	CGDA
Eddie Peabody	DAC#E
Irish	GDAE
Irish Bouzouki	GDAD

Mandolin Banjo

Standard	GDAE

Banjolele *or* Banjo-Ukulele

Standard C6	GCEA
Standard D6	ADF#B

6-String Guitar Banjo

Standard	EADGBE
Drop D	DADGBE
Double Drop D	DADGBD
Dadgad	DADGAD
Open G	DGDGBD

Pony Banjo

Open C	cGCEG

Bass Banjo

Standard	EADG

ALTERNATIVE CHORD NAMES

C	**CM** *or* **Cmaj**
Cm	**Cmin** *or* **C-**
C-5	**C-5** *or* **C(♭5)**
C°	**Cdim**
C4	**Csus4(no 5th)** *or* **Csus(no 5th)**
C5	**C Power Chord** *or* **C(no 3rd)**
Csus2	**C(sus2)** *or* **C2**
Csus4	**Csus** *or* **C(sus4)**
Csus4add9	**Csus(add9)**
C+	**Caug, C+5** *or* **C(♯5)**
C6	**CM6** *or* **CMaj6**
Cadd9	**Cadd2**
Cm6	**C-6** *or* **Cmin6**
Cmadd9	**Cmadd2** *or* **C-(add9)**
C6add9	**C6/9, C$^6_9$** *or* **CMaj6(add9)**
Cm6add9	**Cm6/9** *or* **Cm$^6_9$**
C°7	**Cdim7**
C7	**Cdom**
C7sus2	**C7(sus2)**
C7sus4	**C7sus, C7(sus4)** *or* **Csus11**
C7-5	**C7♭5**
C7+5	**C7+** *or* **C7♯5**
C7-9	**C7♭9** *or* **C7(add♭9)**
C7+9	**C7♯9** *or* **C7(add♯9)**
C7-5-9	**C7♭5♭9**
C7+5-9	**C7♯5♭9**
C7+5+9	**C7♯5♯9**
C7add11	**C7/11** *or* **C$_{11}^7$**
C7+11	**C7♯11**
Cm7	**C-7, Cmi7** *or* **Cmin7**
Cm7-5	**Cm7♭5, C-7-5** *or* **C^ø**
Cm7-5-9	**Cm7♭5♭9**
Cm7-9	**Cm7♭9**
Cm7add11	**Cm**
Cm(maj7)	**Cm♯7, CM7-5, CmM7** *or* **C-△**
Cmaj7	**CM7** *or* **C△(Delta)**
Cmaj7-5	**CM7-5, C△♭5** *or* **Cmaj7♭5**
Cmaj7+5	**CM7+5, C△5+** *or* **Cmaj7♯11**
Cmaj7+11	**CM7+11, C△+♯11** *or* **Cmaj7♯11**
C9	**C7(add9)**
C9sus4	**C9sus** *or* **C9(sus4)**
C9-5	**C9♭5**
C9+5	**C9♯5**
C9+11	**C9♯11**
Cm9	**C-9** *or* **Cmin9**
Cm9-5	**Cm9♭5**
Cm(maj9)	**Cm9(maj7), CmM9** *or* **Cm(addM9)**
Cmaj9	**CM9, Cmaj7(add9), C△9** *or* **CM7(add9)**
Cmaj9-5	**CM9-5, Cmaj9♭5, C△9♭5** *or* **CM9♭5**
Cmaj9+5	**CM9+5, Cmaj9♯5, C△9♯5**
Cmaj9add6	**CM9add6** *or* **C△9add6**
Cmaj9+11	**CM9+11, Cmaj9♯11, C△9♯11** *or* **CM9♯11**
C11	**C7(add11)**
C11-9	**C11♭9**
Cm11	**C-11** *or* **Cmin11**
Cmaj11	**CM11, Cmaj7(add11), C△11, CM7(add11)**
C13	**C7/6(no 9th)** *or* **C7(add13)**
C13sus4	**C13sus** *or* **C13(sus4)**
C13-5-9	**C13♭5♭9**
C13-9	**C13♭9**
C13+9	**C13♯9**
C13+11	**C13♯11** *or* **C13aug11**

Cm13	**C-13** *or* **Cmin13**
Cmaj13	**CM13, Cmaj7(add13),**
	C△13 *or* **CM7(add13)**

M	**major**
m	**minor**
-	**minor**
dim	**diminished**
°	**diminished**
ø	**half diminished**
sus	**suspended**
aug	**augmented**
+	**augmented**
add	**added**
dom	**dominant**
△	**delta /major seventh**
Q(3)	**quartal / double fourth**
♯	**sharp**
×	**double sharp**
♭	**flat**
♭♭	**double flat**

Do	**Spanish for C**
Dó	**Portuguese for C**
Re	**Spanish for D**
Ré	**Portuguese for D**
Mi	**Spanish & Portuguese for E**
Fa	**Spanish & Portuguese for F**
So	**Spanish for G**
Sol	**Portuguese for G**
La	**Spanish for A**
Lá	**Portuguese for A**
Si	**Spanish & Portuguese for B**
H	**German for B**

English Tonic Sol-fa

Do	**C**
Re	**D**
Me	**E**
Fa	**F**
Sol	**G**
La	**A**
Ti	**B**

The majority of music books will use the chords featured in the first column (on the far left and top right), but should you come across alternatives, consult this guide for other naming conventions.

The list above includes most of the symbols and abbreviations that you're likely to encounter in the majority of music books.

NOTES

NOTES

NOTES

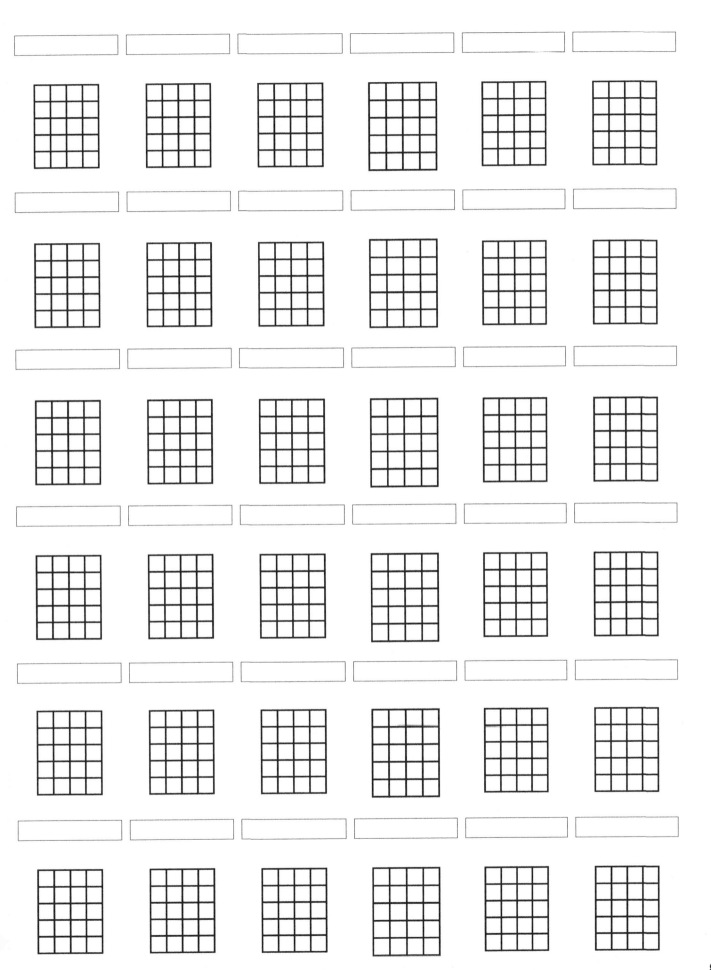

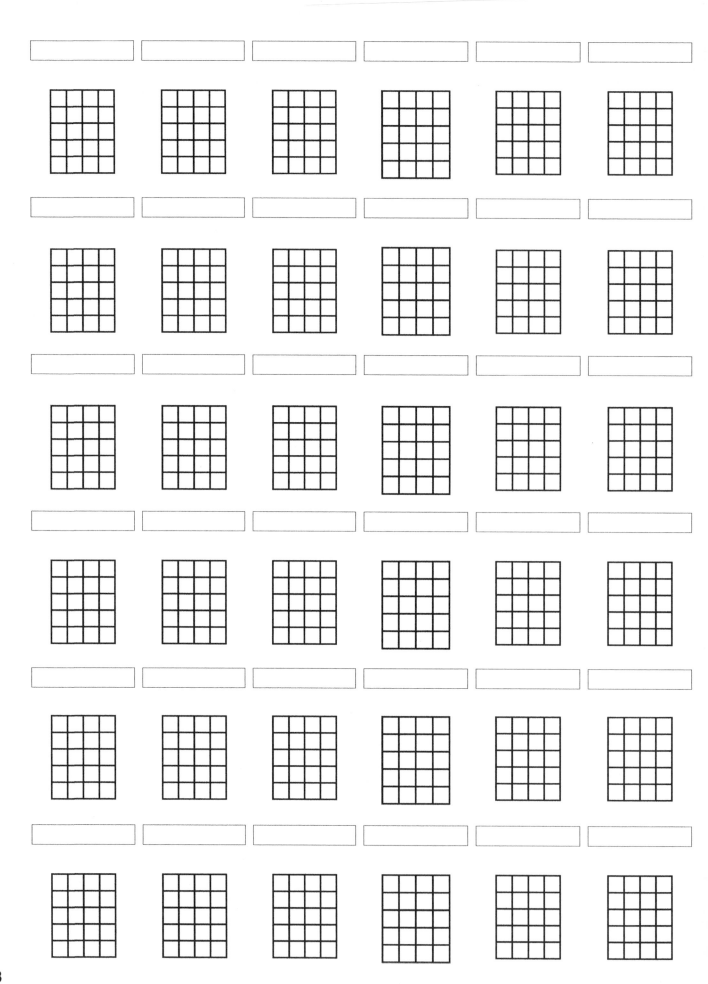

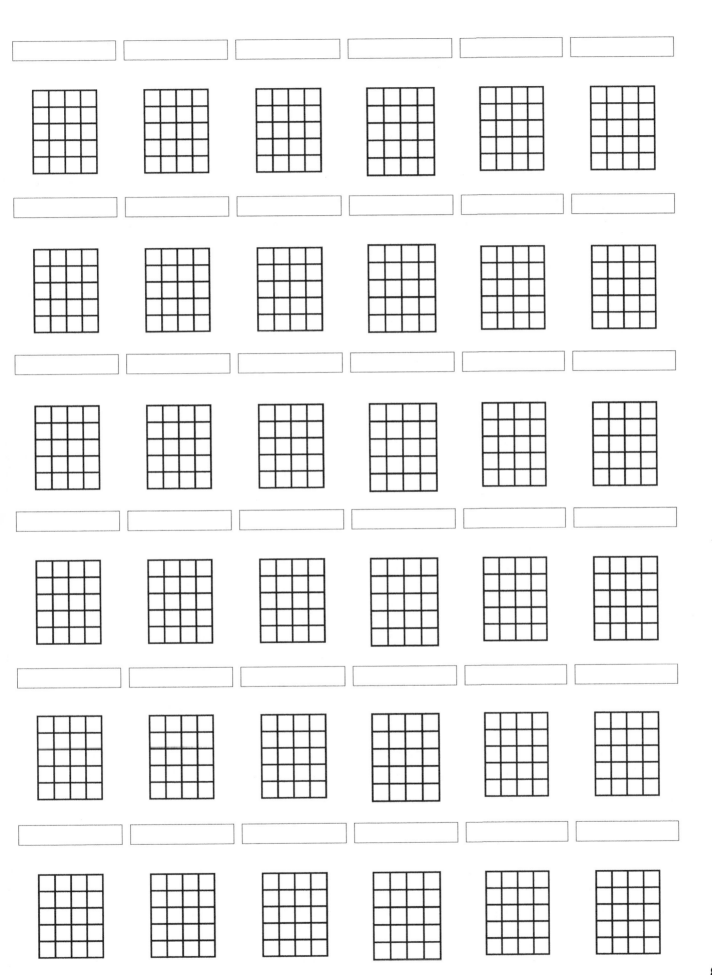

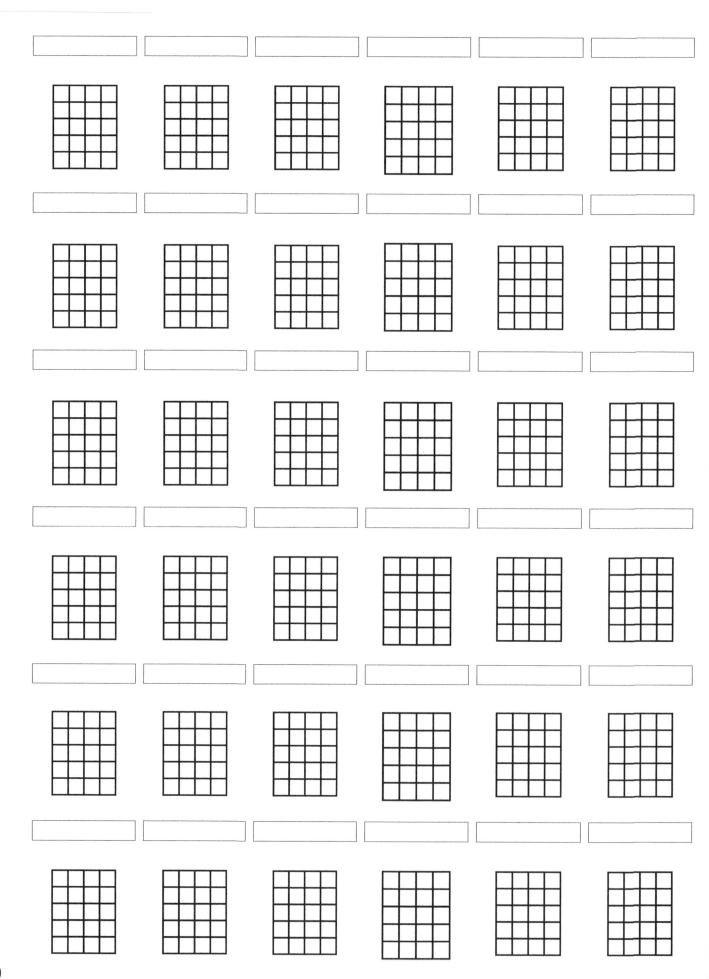

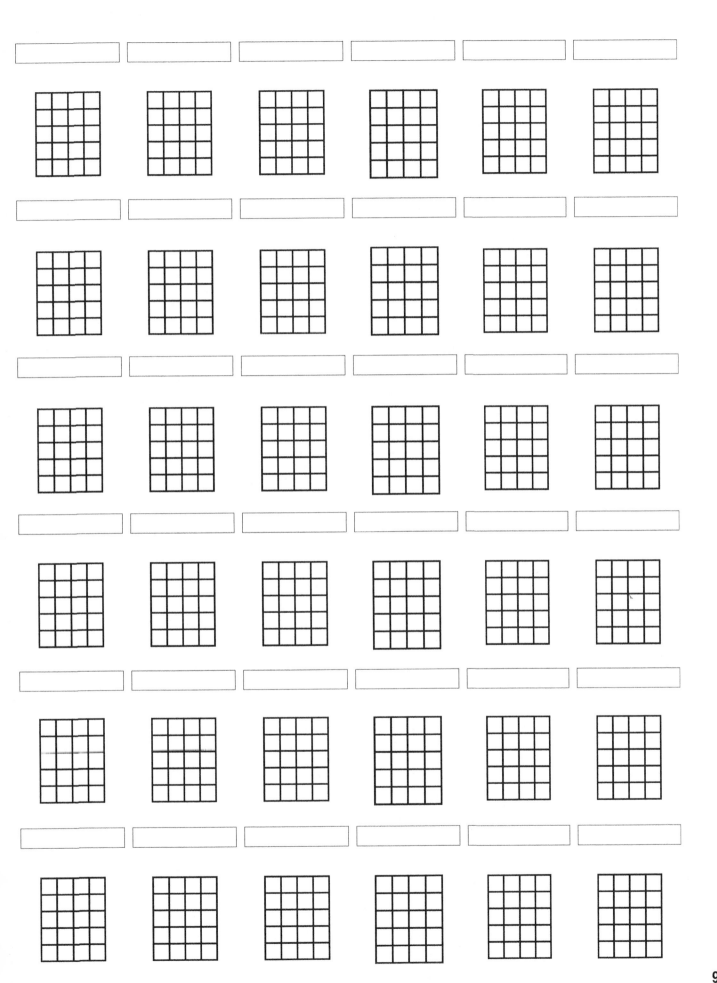

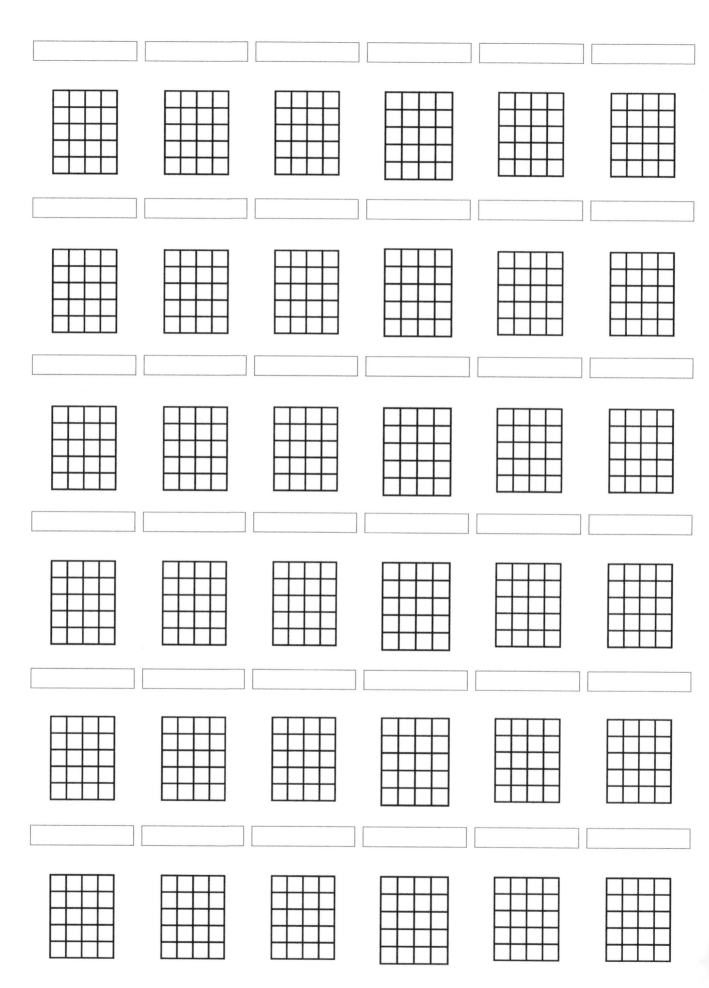

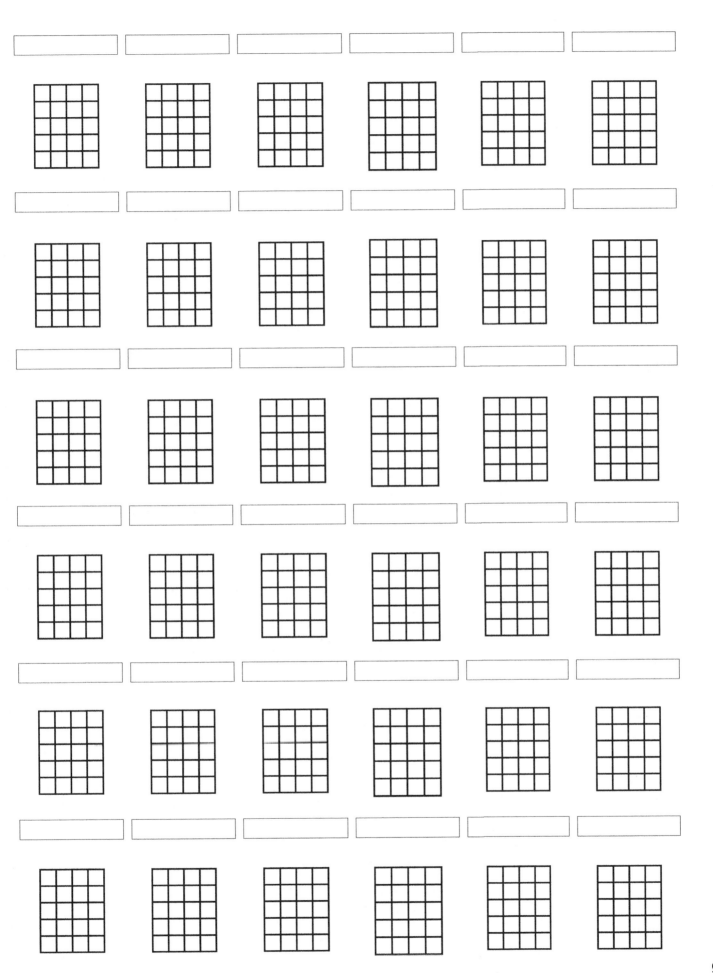

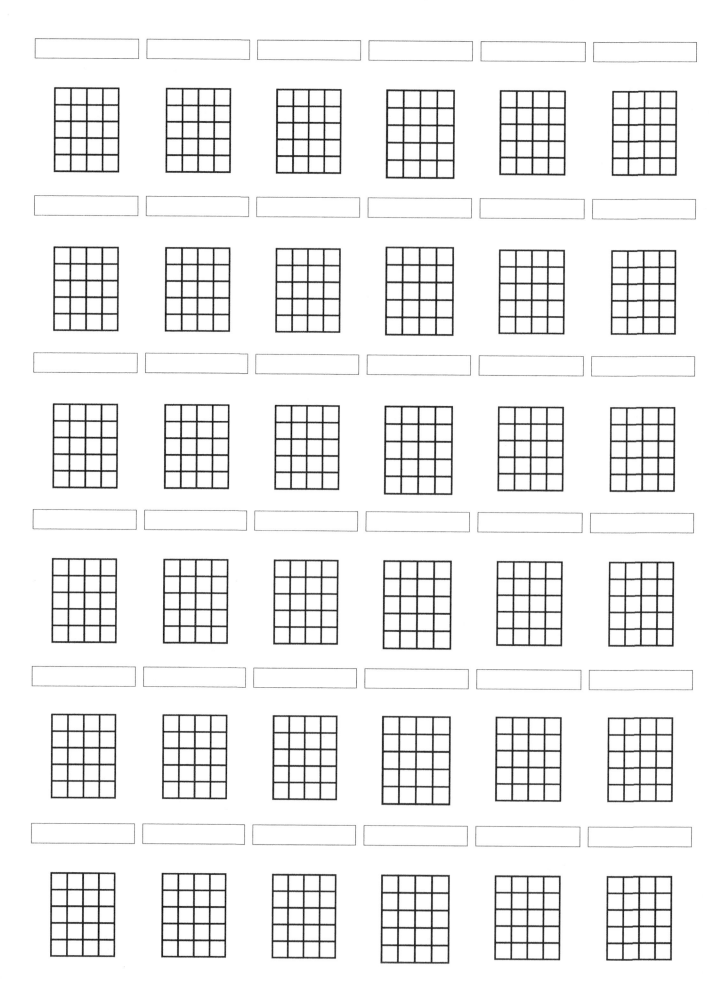

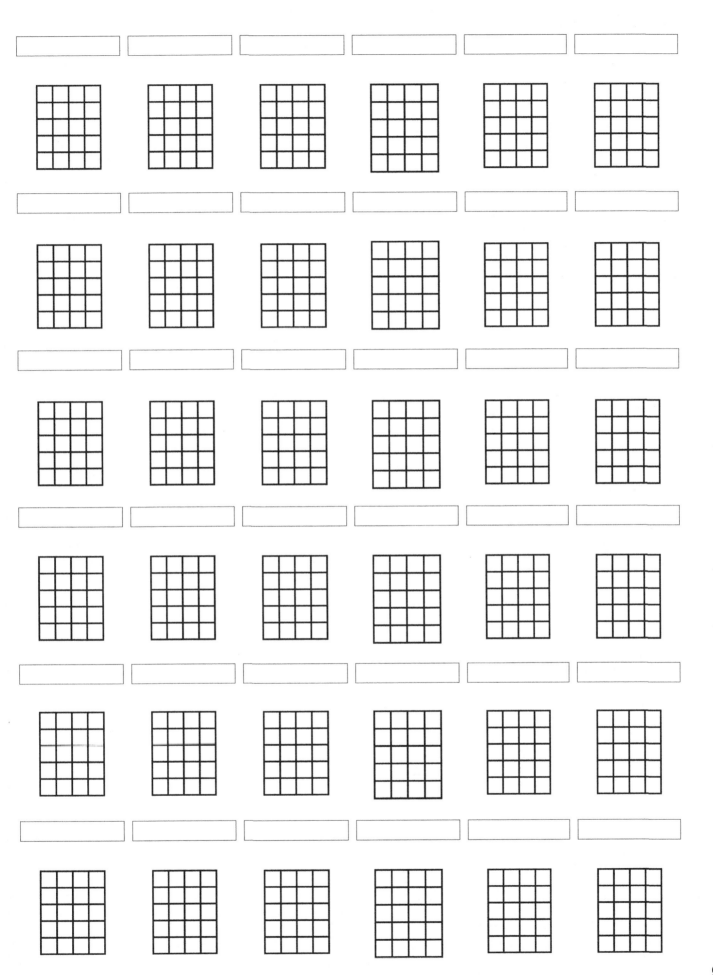

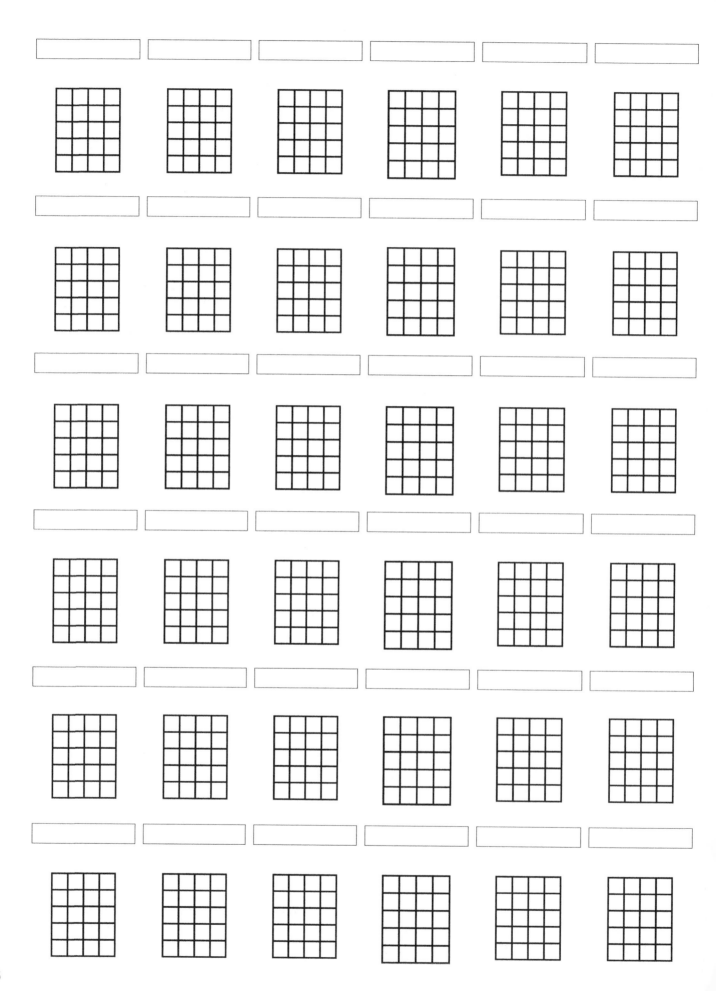

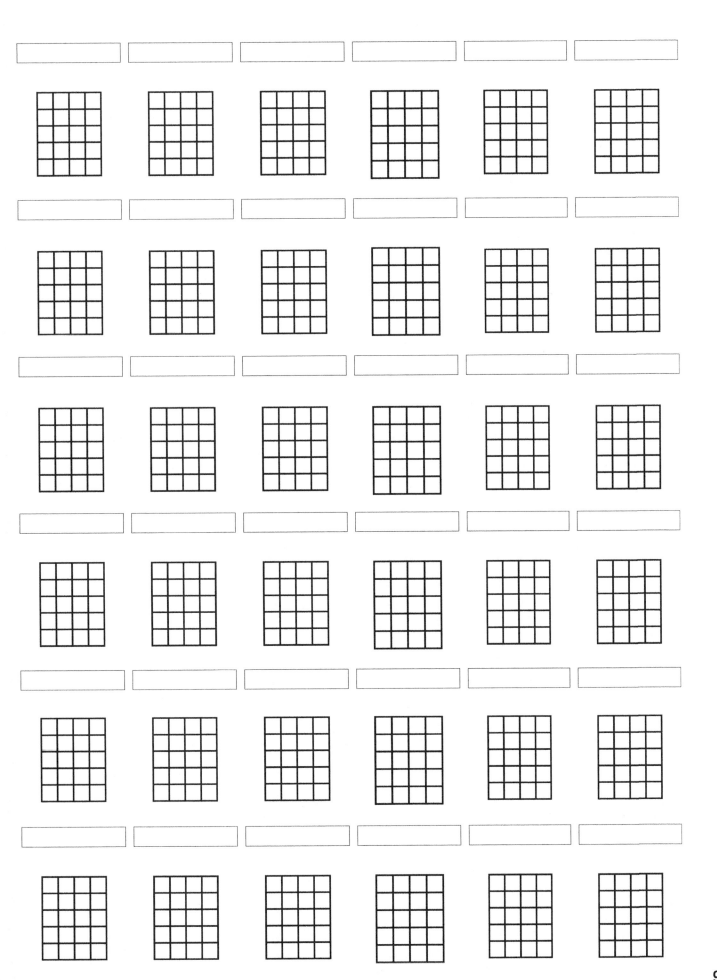

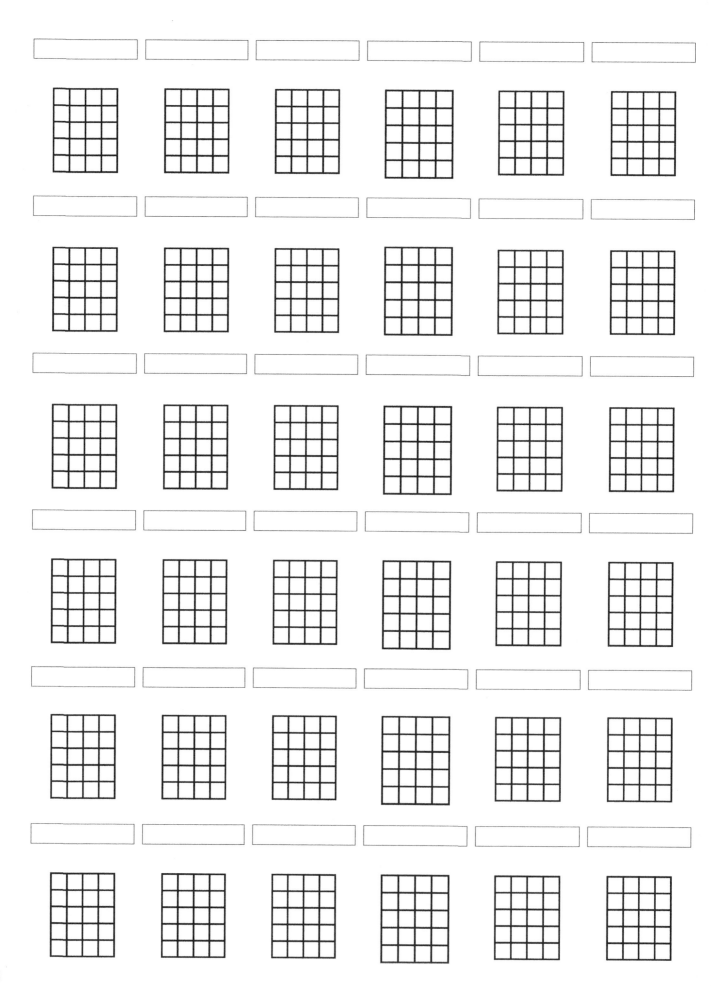

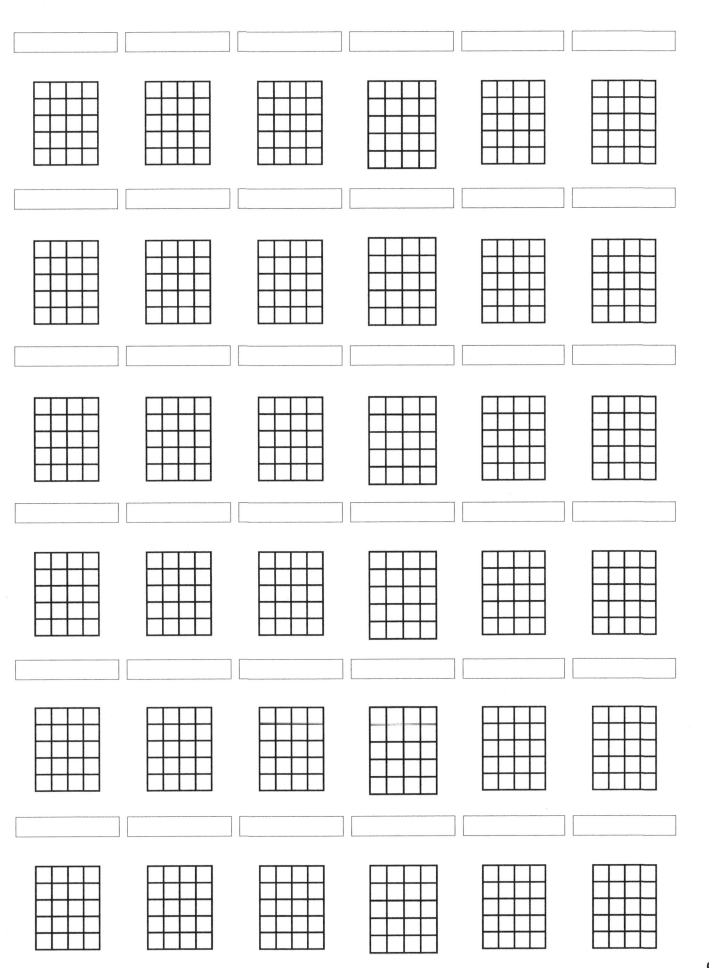

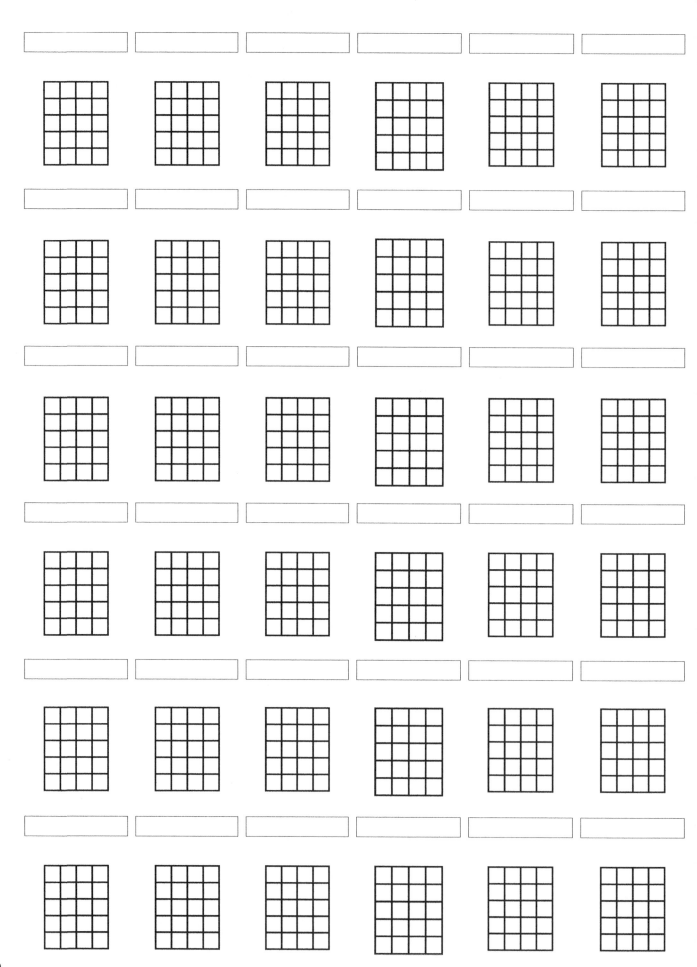

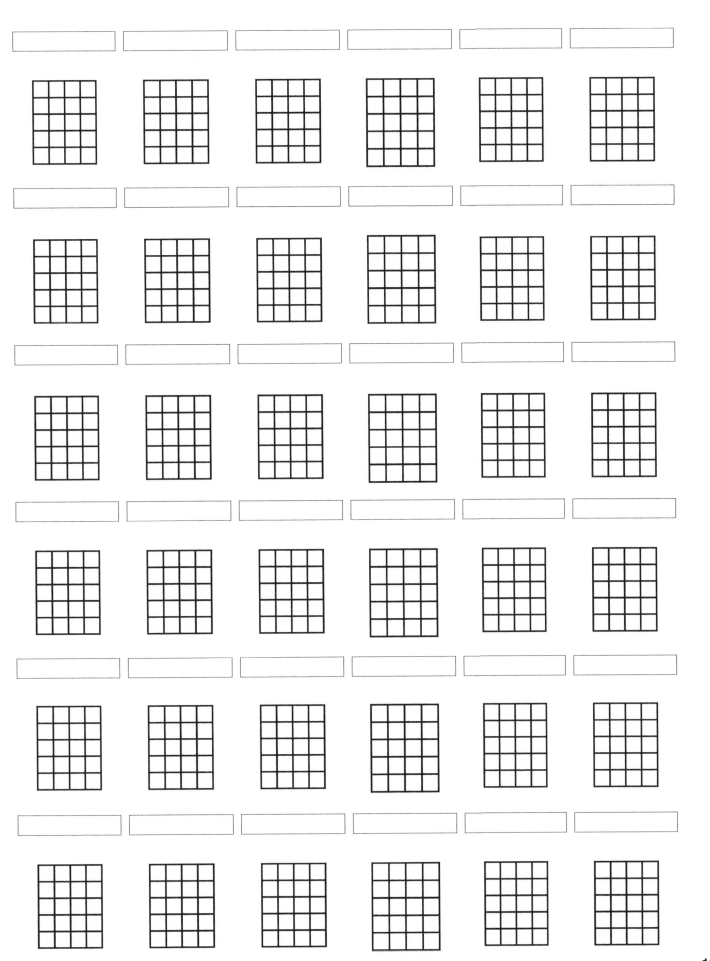

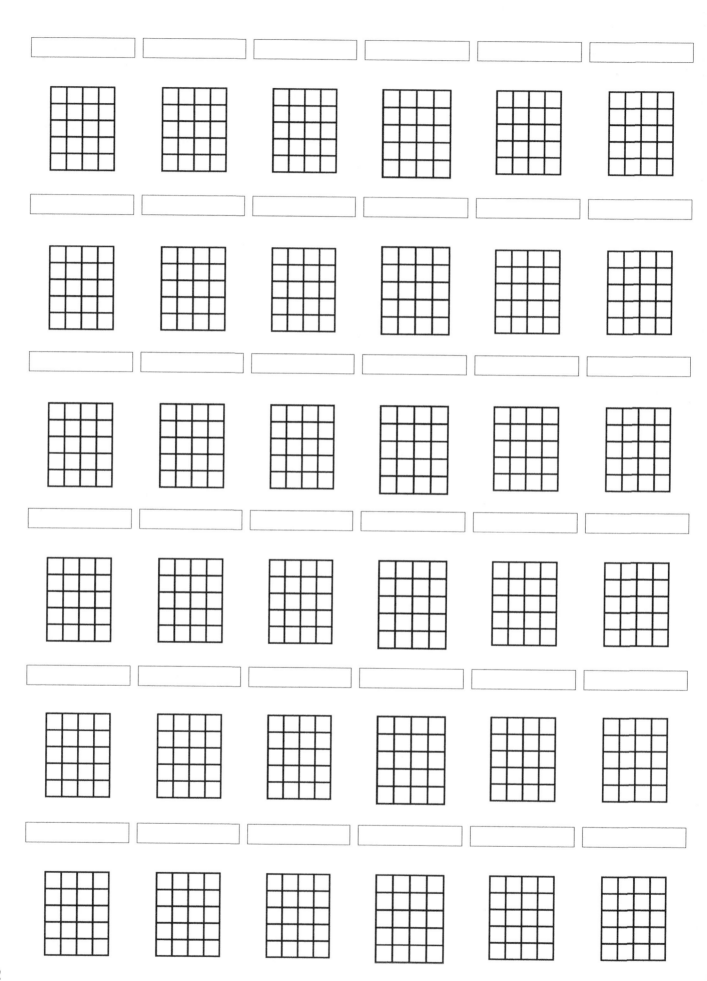

103

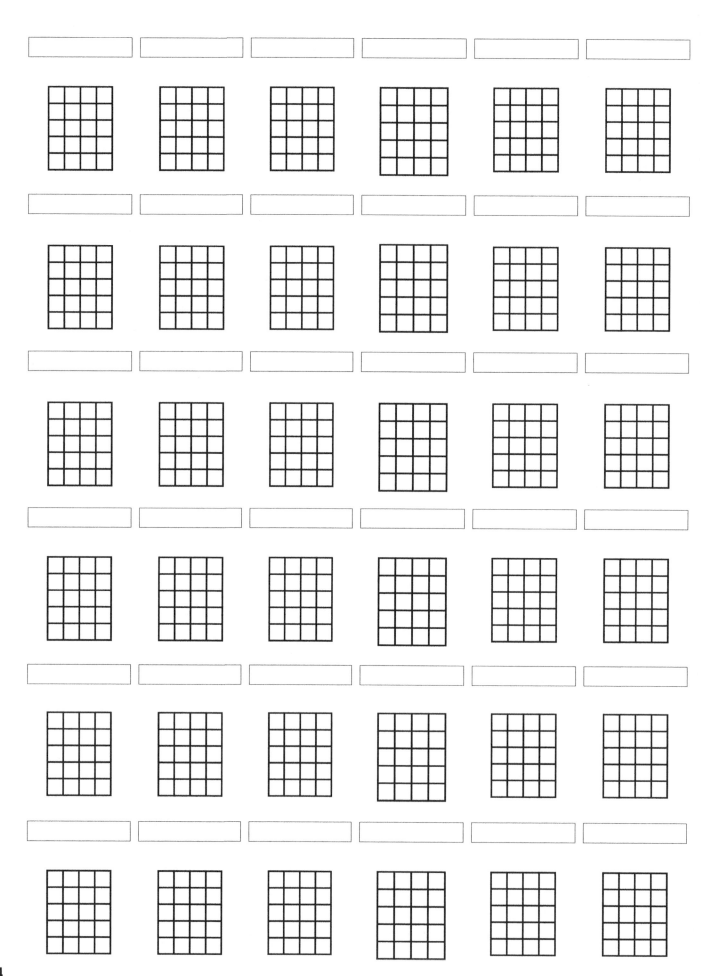

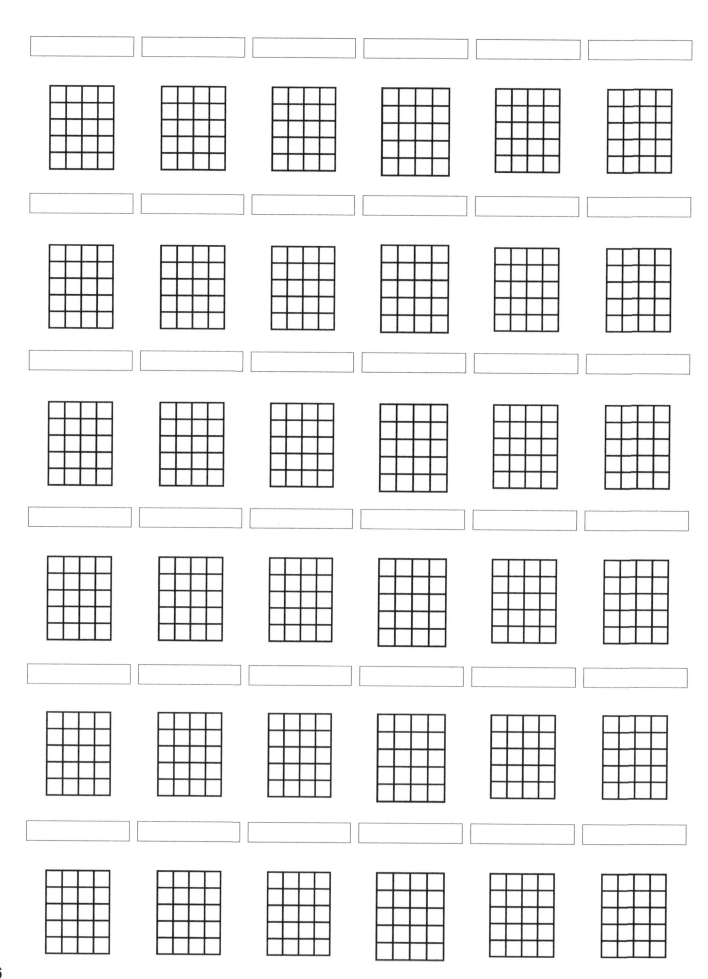

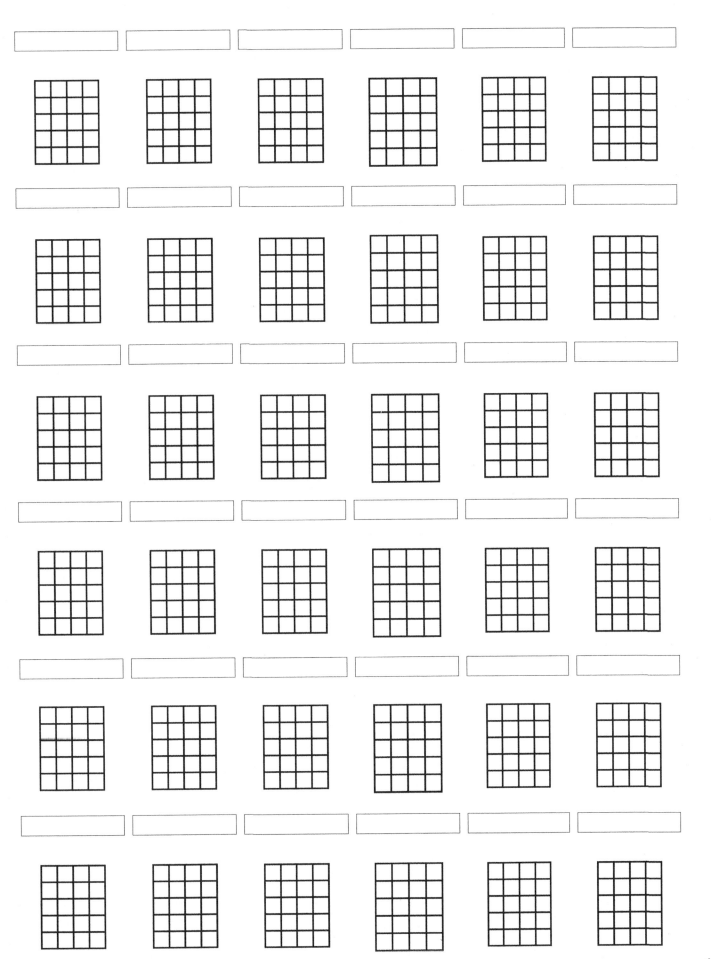

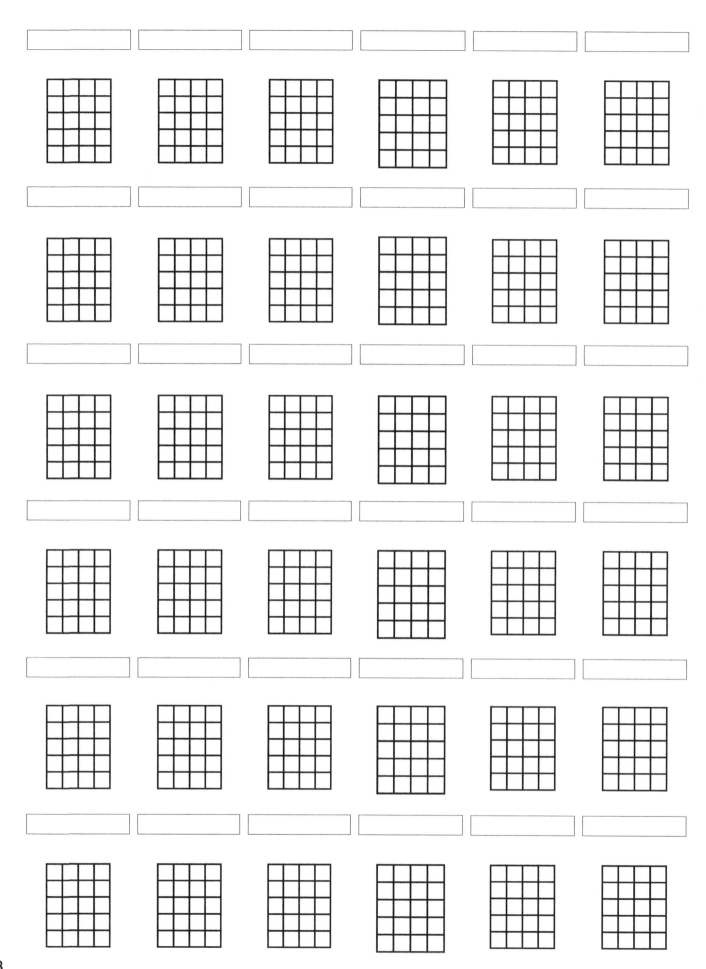

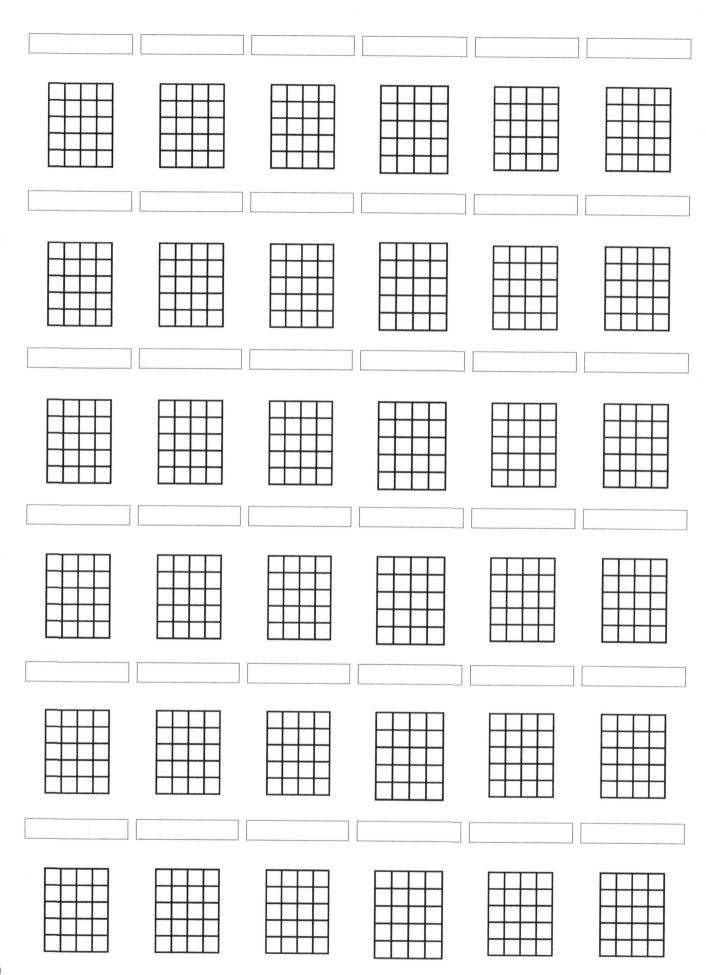

Made in the USA
Middletown, DE
09 September 2022

10017706R00064